Innovative language teaching and learning at university: enhancing participation and collaboration

Edited by Cecilia Goria, Oranna Speicher, and Sascha Stollhans

Research-publishing.net

Published by Research-publishing.net, not-for-profit association
Dublin, Ireland; Voillans, France, info@research-publishing.net

Innovative language teaching and learning at university: enhancing participation and collaboration
Edited by Cecilia Goria, Oranna Speicher, Sascha Stollhans

Typeset by Research-publishing.net
Cover design and frog picture by © Raphaël Savina (raphael@savina.net)

ISBN13: 978-1-908416-31-5 (Paperback - Print on demand, black and white)
Print on demand technology is a high-quality, innovative and ecological printing method; with which the book is
never 'out of stock' or 'out of print'.

ISBN13: 978-1-908416-32-2 (Ebook, PDF, colour)
ISBN13: 978-1-908416-33-9 (Ebook, EPUB, colour)

Legal deposit, Ireland: The National Library of Ireland, The Library of Trinity College, The Library of the
University of Limerick, The Library of Dublin City University, The Library of NUI Cork, The Library of NUI
Maynooth, The Library of University College Dublin, The Library of NUI Galway.

Legal deposit, United Kingdom: The British Library.
British Library Cataloguing-in-Publication Data.
A cataloguing record for this book is available from the British Library.

Legal deposit, France: Bibliothèque Nationale de France - Dépôt légal: janvier 2016.

Table of contents

Table of contents

Notes on contributors

Editors

Cecilia **Goria** is a Lecturer of Italian in the Language Centre, University of Nottingham. She also lectures in general Linguistics and she is the academic director of the distance learning MA in Digital Technologies for Language Teaching. Cecilia has a strong research background in Theoretical Linguistics and in recent years her research interests have shifted towards the area of Distance Learning and Online Open Pedagogies, with a specific focus on Language Teaching and Learning.

Oranna **Speicher** has an MA in Linguistics and Language Teaching (Leeds) and is a part-time PhD student (Nottingham). She is an experienced language teacher of both English and German, and her teaching experience covers secondary schools, adult education and the HE sector. Her research interests are technology-enhanced language teaching and learning, second language acquisition, and language pedagogy. Currently, she is the Director of the Language Centre at the University of Nottingham.

Sascha **Stollhans** has a BA in German Linguistics and French Studies and an MA in German as a Foreign Language (Berlin). He has taught German at universities and language schools in Germany, South Africa, France and the UK. In 2012/2013 he worked as a tutor appointed via the DAAD (German Academic Exchange Service) and as a teacher on a pre-ITT (Initial Teacher Training) course at Newcastle University, before he joined the University of Nottingham as a DAAD-Lektor in 2013. His main teaching and research areas are German language and linguistics, applied linguistics, second language acquisition, and language pedagogy.

Invited contributors

Jan **Hardman** is a Lecturer in Language Education in the Department of Education at University of York, United Kingdom. She lectures in Applied

Linguistics, TESOL and Language Education. She conducts research into classroom discourse and interaction, dialogic pedagogy and teacher education. She has been involved in a number of individual and collaborative research projects and has published journal articles and peer-reviewed book chapters. Informed by her research, Jan contributes to staff professional development courses on teaching and learning in higher education and schools.

Zoltán **Dörnyei** is Professor of Psycholinguistics at the School of English, University of Nottingham. He has published nearly 100 academic papers and book chapters on various aspects of language learner characteristics, second language acquisition and language teaching methodology, and he is the author of over 20 books, including Research Methods in Applied Linguistics (2007, Oxford University Press), The Psychology of Second Language Acquisition (2009, Oxford University Press), Motivating Learners, Motivating Teachers: Building Vision in the Language Classroom (2014, Cambridge University Press, with M. Kubanyiova), The Psychology of The Language Learner Revisited (2015, Routledge, with S. Ryan) and Motivational Currents in Language Learning: Frameworks for Focused Interventions (2016, Routledge, with A. Henry & C. Muir).

Contributors

Carmen **Álvarez-Mayo** is a Spanish Associate Lecturer and Coordinator in Languages for All at the University of York. Since October 2015, she has contributed to the development of FL courses, the curricula, learning and assessment materials and the VLE; as well as the Spanish L&LS degree and marketing materials. She is also a Spanish Lecturer at Leeds Beckett University and has worked at Instituto Cervantes in Manchester and Leeds. Carmen loves learning and her main interests are New Media, developing learning and teaching materials, Non-Verbal Communication and Equality & Diversity Issues. She also works as a translator, interpreter, editor and voiceover actor.

Fakhreddine **Brahmi** has an MA degree in Didactics of English, has been a teacher and head of exam juries at the department of English, University of Gafsa, Tunisia for 10 years. He holds TKT, TOIEC trainer, TESOL, and Learning Technologies for the Classroom certificates, among many others. He has also taught English to adult learners who are interested in getting internationally recognised certificates. He translated and contributed reporting to The New York Times. His interests are didactics, digital learning, assessment, CPD, and writing poetry.

Anna (Ania) **de Berg** is Senior Lecturer in German, and Language Centre Coordinator at Sheffield Hallam University. Before joining Hallam, she taught and conducted research at universities in Germany, Poland, Austria and the UK, including the Universities of York, Leeds Beckett and Sheffield. Her publications include *Verbalisierung und Visualisierung der Erinnerung, Literatur und Medien in Österreich* (co-ed., 2008) and *"Nach Galizien", Entwicklung der Reiseliteratur am Beispiel der deutschsprachigen Reiseberichte vom 18. bis zum 21. Jahrhundert* (2010). In recent years, her research interest has shifted towards intercultural communication and use of digital media in MFL teaching.

Ariane **Demeure-Ahearne** is the French Language Co-ordinator in the SMLC, and has responsibility for Year Abroad placements. She has particular interests in e-learning, language learning pedagogy and the student experience. Recent projects include the development of online language learning resources for Year Abroad students and a language-teaching training programme for post-graduates.

Filippo **Gilardi** is an Assistant Professor in Culture, Languages and Digital Media at The University of Nottingham, Ningbo, China. His current research interests focus on the notions of Transmedia Storytelling and Participatory Culture, looking at how these concepts influence the way we are teaching and learning through blogs, wikis, social networks and other virtual spaces. Apart from teaching and researching, he co-founded two start-ups: www.pubcoder. com and www.transmediaeducation.org, the former with the purpose to facilitate publishing digital stories, the latter to improve teachers and students technological skills.

Cathy **Hampton** is principal teaching fellow in the French section of the School of Modern Languages and Cultures (SMLC) at Warwick University. Her research interests lie in higher education pedagogy and the student experience, and e learning. Recent projects have focused on the Year Abroad student experience and the notion of ethical engagement.

Insa **Hartung** is DAAD-Lektorin at the University of St Andrews. She has a background in translation and holds a Master in Teaching German as a Foreign Language from the Humboldt University of Berlin. At St Andrews, she teaches German at all levels, with a special interest in the use of technology and translation in foreign language teaching. More recently, she has also been working on teaching materials for CEFR level C2 language learners. Another research interest is in task-based and collaborative learning and teaching.

Neil **Hughes** is Director of Modern Language Teaching at the University of Nottingham. He teaches Spanish language on both the Spanish undergraduate and the Inter-Faculty institution-wide programmes and offers a module to final-year Spanish students entitled: Business and Society in Contemporary Spain. His research interests lie in two disciplines: political economy and language education. In his most recent publication in the field of political economy, published in the International Journal of Community Currency Research, he maps the community currency scene in Spain. In education, he is particularly interested in both blended language learning and teaching and the delivery of content-based modules through the medium of Spanish.

Mizuho **Jones** teaches Japanese at the University of Nottingham, Ningbo, China. Her main area of interest is the effects of technology on language teaching.

Lan **Lo** obtained a PhD in Contemporary Chinese studies from the University of Nottingham. Her interests encompass two areas: Chinese migrant communities in the UK and Chinese Language Teaching. She has been developing an international research profile with publications of a co-authored book, two journal articles, two in press, and papers accepted and presented at five international conferences, most recently presentations on Blended Learning in Chinese at Bath and Leeds University. She is participating in a large bid to AHRC OWRI research grant in the School of Cultures, Languages and Area Studies (lead on Nottingham Chinese strand), University of Nottingham.

Joaquin **Lopez** has been teaching at the University of Nottingham, Ningbo, China since 2005. His teaching and research focuses mainly on modern languages, comparative literature and cultural studies.

Sandra **López-Rocha** is a teaching fellow at the University of Bristol with a background in sociolinguistics, intercultural communication, ethnography of communication, and social anthropology. Her research focuses on language maintenance, ethnic identity, and intercultural adaptation. She has worked at the University of Maryland Baltimore County and in various projects with the University of Jyväskylä, Finland. She currently coordinates Year Abroad Work Placements in Spanish-speaking countries at the UoB, which has allowed her to observe and act on the difficulties that students experience involving intercultural adaptation and communicative competence. She continues to research intercultural and sociolinguistic issues in multicultural settings.

Born in France and raised in Austria, Hanna **Magedera-Hofhansl** did a degree in French, Portuguese and Lutheran theology at the universities of Vienna and Strasbourg. She came to the University of Liverpool in 2001 as a Lektorin der Österreich Kooperation (now Österreichischer Austauschdienst) and is now a Lecturer in German Language and Business German as well as Translation.

Anna **Motzo** is a Lecturer in Italian at the Open University. Areas of interest are the development of language learning materials within a technology-enhanced environment and the wider role of e-learning in the democratisation of culture. She has authored articles on OERs, dyslexia friendly language resources and peer e-mentoring.

Elinor **Parks** is a PhD student in Applied Linguistics at the University of Hull. She is also a part-time lecturer of German and Italian at Leeds Beckett University. Her doctoral research explores the complexity behind the separation between language and content in Modern Language degrees both in the UK and in the USA. In particular, the research examines implications of the divide for the development of criticality and intercultural competence in undergraduates. She has presented at a number of conferences around the UK including Southampton, Liverpool, Sheffield, Leeds and Nottingham.

Alessia **Plutino** is a teaching fellow of Italian at the University of Southampton and an Associate Lecturer at The Open University. She has multiple research interests ranging from Computer Assisted Language Learning and Telecollaboration to the use of microblogging (Twitter) to enhance communicative language learning and accuracy. All her projects have a focus on cultural and intercultural awareness, and this is also the case for the academically led trip to Italy scheme (Italy DIY), which she designed and implemented to enhance students' employability and independent skills, as well as creating opportunities for students to become content producers of OERs.

Salim **Razı** is an Assistant Professor at the English Language Teaching Department of Canakkale Onsekiz Mart University, Turkey, where he trains EFL teachers and offers graduate courses. He has published papers on nativization and cultural schema, metacognitive reading strategies, teaching and assessing reading, teaching and assessing academic writing, detecting and avoiding plagiarism, listening activities, teaching culture and intercultural communicative competence, and research culture. He has recently developed a model to teach academic writing by means of providing effective peer feedback in an online environment, and has been awarded the Turnitin Global Innovation Awards in 2015.

James **Reid** is a Lecturer in the English for Academic Purposes (EAP) department of Akita International University, Japan. Prior to this appointment, he taught EAP courses at The University of Nottingham, Ningbo, China, and at a private college in the UK. He has published a number of papers on the use of transmedia storytelling in education and entertainment, and regularly conducts workshops that use the transmedia storytelling concept to develop collaborative learning projects. Based on the results of this research, he is now investigating the balance between direct instruction and social-constructivism in the promotion of intrinsic and extrinsic motivation.

Sandra **Reisenleutner** is a Teaching Associate at the University of Nottingham. She previously worked at the University of Sheffield and at the University of St Andrews as OEAD-Lektorin. Her research interests lie in developing teaching material for the various levels of the CEFR, in task-based teaching and learning as well as in collaboration in the language classroom. She also works on how to incorporate digital tools in foreign language learning.

Dorota **Rzycka** teaches French at the University of Nottingham, Ningbo, China. She has a doctorate in Francophone Literature. Apart from research on formation of (multi-)cultural identity, her professional interests focus on the role of technology in language teaching and learning.

Marion **Sadoux** is currently the Director of the Language Centre at the University of Nottingham, Ningbo, China where she also acts as Academic Director of Online Learning. Marion teaches an accredited Work Placement in the Language Centre module for Chinese and International undergraduate students as well as Second Language Acquisition and Teaching, an online module for the MA in Digital Technologies for Language Teaching. She is involved in a number of University wide projects under the umbrella of Students as Change Agents.

Foreword

Zoltán Dörnyei[1]

Most universities, domestic and international alike, place some emphasis on the knowledge of foreign languages, because in the globalised environment of the contemporary world, intercultural communication has come to be seen as an indispensable requirement for the 'global citizen'. University students usually aspire to qualify for this title, and even in English-speaking countries where home students speak Global English as their first language, there is a recognition of the advantages of being able to relate to people from other ethnolinguistic communities in their own language. Accordingly, university students tend to be positively inclined towards engaging in some form of L2 instruction, provided it is offered in an effective and efficient manner. This condition is central to the subject of this volume: because for most university students – even for those who study modern foreign languages – the actual proficiency of the L2 is primarily a vehicle for dealing with various content areas associated with the subject matter of their studies, L2 instruction cannot be successful if it takes up too much of the learners' available time and effort. That is, in the competition for the students' attention at university level, foreign language teaching is bound to lose out unless L2 teachers can come up with innovative ways of delivering L2 instruction that provides good value in an engaging form.

As its title suggests, *Innovative language teaching and learning at university: enhancing participation and collaboration* presents a principled attempt to address the issue of how L2 instruction at university level can meet such heightened demands. The Editors served as the organisers of a successful conference at the School of Cultures, Languages and Area Studies

1. University of Nottingham, Nottingham, United Kingdom; zoltan.dornyei@nottingham.ac.uk

How to cite: Dörnyei, Z. (2016). Foreword. In C. Goria, O. Speicher, & S. Stollhans (Eds), *Innovative language teaching and learning at university: enhancing participation and collaboration* (pp. xiii-xv). Dublin: Research-publishing.net. http://dx.doi.org/10.14705/rpnet.2016.000398

at The University of Nottingham, *'InnoConf 2015'*, where the rich programme specifically focused on various novel ways of exploring the benefits of state-of-the-art instructional approaches, such as the use of technology and the Internet, content-based language learning, the development of intercultural communicative competence/awareness, different study-abroad schemes and field trips, as well as utilising certain key psychological processes underlying institutional learning such as learner autonomy and motivation. The current volume offers a good selection of papers representing three main themes: online collaboration, digital tools in online environments and teaching that goes beyond the boundaries of the language classroom.

There is no doubt that this is an interesting and ambitious volume with a rich content, and I have found two aspects of the contributions particularly noteworthy. First of all, they provide convincing evidence of the wide array of effective teaching tools that are at the disposal of any L2 practitioner who would like to go beyond using traditional methodologies – and indeed, the general finding of the chapters, namely that university students are eager to embrace innovative methods if they can sense their pragmatic usefulness, is highly encouraging. It does not come as a surprise that in our current technological age, the Internet and related digital solutions lead the way on the front of innovation; one does not need to have prophetic skills to predict that online, virtual learning environments will play a growing role in L2 instruction over the decades to come. However, we must not forget that whatever form technology takes, it will always remain merely the channel of student engagement, and the driving engine of such engagement is the students' *motivation*, that is, the extent to which technology-based techniques can capture the students' interest. Therefore, I particularly welcome the effort evident in virtually all the chapters of the current volume to present techniques that explore aspects of e-learning and media skills in close cooperation with motivational considerations and strategies.

The second important aspect of the studies in this volume concerns their research-based nature. L2 instructors working within university environments constitute the segment of the language teaching profession that is probably most aware of the significance of systematic, evidence-based approaches, as these professionals are part of the overall academic climate which highlights the need to support one's claims with some kind of data-based proof. The chapters in this book represent a variety of methodologies in this respect, but they share in common the fact that the innovative techniques and learning arrangements are described in terms of their impact on *real* university language learners. Although the authors draw on experiences from diverse international contexts, there is a great deal of transferable content across the various institutional and national boundaries, and it is safe to claim that every reader is likely to find useful material in the papers that is relevant to their own teaching needs.

Finally on a personal note, I was pleased to see that aspects of *project-based learning* have been incorporated in several chapters. In my own research I have come to increasingly believe that the key to developing long-term motivation is to generate 'directed motivational currents' – see *Motivational Currents in Language Learning: Frameworks for Focused Interventions* (Dörnyei, Z., Henry, A. & Muir, C.; Routledge, 2016) – and one of the best ways of producing such currents in institutional learning contexts is through the engagement with an extended project. Whether a project is aimed at enhancing a study-abroad experience or promoting student collaboration across institutions, the goal-oriented and action-based framework that typically characterises learning projects can offer an instructional mechanism that is highly effective in supporting and sustaining student engagement over longer periods, thereby energising the extended learning behaviour required for the mastery of a foreign language.

In conclusion, I commend this volume warmly to anybody who is looking for ways of 'spicing up' language teaching in university contexts. As an applied linguist myself, I fully appreciate the genuinely applied nature of the content, characterised by a successful combination of theoretical and practical insights and considerations. The chapters present the voices of language practitioners who have not been content to allow language teaching to take a marginal place in higher education but were ready to take risks and aim higher, wishing to educate multilingual citizens of the global world. I do hope that through their sharing techniques and approaches that have worked for their own students, many other colleagues will find inspiration in a range of higher education institutions.

1 "Innovative language teaching and learning at university: enhancing participation and collaboration" – an introduction

Cecilia Goria[1], Oranna Speicher[2], and Sascha Stollhans[3]

The School of Cultures, Languages and Area Studies at the University of Nottingham was delighted to host the annual conference in the series *Innovative Language Teaching and Learning at University* in 2015. The inaugural conference took place in 2010 at Newcastle University, and the conference is now in its fifth year.

This year's conference theme of *Innovative Language Teaching and Learning at University: Enhancing Participation and Collaboration* saw a varied programme of 24 parallel sessions, which broadly fall into three categories: *fostering online collaboration, exploring digital tools and online environments*, and thirdly *beyond the language classroom*.

We were fortunate to be able to welcome as our keynote speakers Professor Zoltán Dörnyei, who wrote the foreword to this edited volume, and Dr Jan Hardman, who also contributed a short article on *Opening-up classroom discourse to promote and enhance active, collaborative and cognitively-engaging student learning experience*. She argues for the creation of a dialogic space in the language classroom, which can then be filled with high-quality classroom interaction which serves as a highly effective tool for fostering students' active learning.

---

1. University of Nottingham, Nottingham, United Kingdom; cecilia.goria@nottingham.ac.uk

2. University of Nottingham, Nottingham, United Kingdom; oranna.speicher@nottingham.ac.uk

3. University of Nottingham, Nottingham, United Kingdom; sascha.stollhans@nottingham.ac.uk

How to cite this chapter: Goria, C., Speicher, O., & Stollhans, S. (2016). "Innovative language teaching and learning at university: enhancing participation and collaboration" – an introduction. In C. Goria, O. Speicher, & S. Stollhans (Eds), *Innovative language teaching and learning at university: enhancing participation and collaboration* (pp. 1-4). Dublin: Research-publishing.net. http://dx.doi.org/10.14705/rpnet.2016.000399

In addition to Jan Hardman's keynote paper, 15 conference papers are published in this volume. The contributions under the heading *Fostering online collaboration* have at their core the principle of getting students to work together on and for a common aim and result. First, Motzo shares her experience of an online buddy scheme involving students on a distance learning degree which highlights the importance of collaboration and support amongst off-campus students. Hartung and Reisenleutner then report on an innovative project that partnered students of German at two UK universities using the online tool *Voicethread*. Students worked cooperatively and collaboratively to produce a virtual travel guide to their respective university town. A further example of student partnerships is illustrated in Álvarez-Mayo's contribution, who reports on an online exchange between a group of students based in Spain and a second group of students based in the UK. In the final paper in this section, Razı focusses on collaboration in the area of feedback, in particular the differences between open and anonymous peer feedback.

The selected short papers in the second section deal with *Exploring digital tools and online environments*. De Berg's paper describes a project where students of German Business, Society and Culture were given an opportunity to develop their digital literacy skills alongside their language and cultural studies. The social networking site Facebook and a wiki are at the centre of Brahmi's project: the paper reports on a study involving students of English and their perceptions of using social media to improve their English writing skills. Magedera-Hofhansl presents an innovative project which focusses on all four skills and gives students the opportunity to "become a reporter". Reid and Gilardi's contribution reports on a project involving Japanese learners of academic writing in English and the results of the introduction of the transmedia teaching method to challenge the prevailing paradigm of passive consumers of knowledge amongst the students. The section concludes with the paper by Sadoux, Rzycka, Jones, and Lopez, which describes the implementation of a new navigational structure for their institution's virtual learning environment. The innovative aspect of this structure, which is based on distributive learning, lies in the fact that it was designed by students.

The third and final section of this volume, *Beyond the language classroom*, brings together six papers that share a focus on cultural aspects of language learning. Hampton and Demeure-Ahearne give an account of a partnership project between year abroad students and local widening participation schools, where the students used digital tools not only to create teaching and learning materials for the students in their local schools, but also online spaces, such as blogs, to reflect on their year abroad experience and the development of their intercultural competence. Staying with the theme of intercultural competence, López-Rocha highlights the need for teachers to create language courses that facilitate the acquisition of intercultural competence, as well as the challenges such inclusion into the curriculum brings. The benefits of field trips for modern languages students are discussed by Plutino who reports on a group of ab initio Italian learners and the associated benefits for motivation, engagement and collaboration. The next two papers cover the area of Content and Language Integrated Learning (CLIL): Parks looks at the complex relationship between language and culture and compares UK and US higher education with regards to the development of intercultural competence; Hughes discusses the implications of subject discipline content being delivered through a second language, and reflects on how language departments in the UK are dealing with the question as to whether subject content should be delivered in the foreign language or in English. The final paper by Lo highlights the challenges Cantonese speakers face in Mandarin classes and reports on a case study investigating those students' needs, motivations and barriers regarding the learning of Mandarin.

The year-on-year increase in the number of contributors and delegates attending this conference series is testament to the need for this type of event, where researchers and practitioners in language teaching and learning come together to share best practices and find colleagues for collaboration, both nationally and internationally.

To conclude, we would like to express our appreciation to the presenters and delegates, without whom there would be no conference. Also, we would like to thank our School of Cultures, Languages and Area Studies here at the University of Nottingham as well as Sanako for sponsoring the event. The conference was expertly hosted by our student ambassadors, and we greatly appreciate their help and enthusiasm for the event. Finally, we would like to express our gratitude to Sylvie Thouësny and Karine Fenix at Research-publishing.net, for their excellent support throughout the publishing process of this edited volume. Their efficiency, support and professionalism is second to none.

2 Opening-up classroom discourse to promote and enhance active, collaborative and cognitively-engaging student learning experiences

Jan Hardman[1]

Abstract

This paper places classroom discourse and interaction right at the heart of the teaching and learning process. It is built on the argument that high quality talk between the teacher and student(s) provides a fertile ground for an active, highly collaborative and cognitively stimulating learning process leading to improved learning outcomes. High quality classroom talk is characterised by the use of open and authentic questions and formative feedback whereby student contributions are probed and elaborated on. An example of this is illustrated in a detailed transcript analysis of an extract of classroom discourse derived from a university seminar. It is argued that there is a need to create dialogic space and open up classroom discourse to enhance students' active learning, particularly in language classrooms.

Keywords: classroom discourse, teacher-student interaction, dialogic teaching, collaborative learning, language learning.

1. University of York, York, United Kingdom; jan.hardman@york.ac.uk

How to cite this chapter: Hardman, J. (2016). Opening-up classroom discourse to promote and enhance active, collaborative and cognitively-engaging student learning experiences. In C. Goria, O. Speicher, & S. Stollhans (Eds), *Innovative language teaching and learning at university: enhancing participation and collaboration* (pp. 5-16). Dublin: Research-publishing.net. http://dx.doi.org/10.14705/rpnet.2016.000400

1.   Introduction

Research has shown that classroom interaction is central to teaching and learning, not only functioning as a pedagogical tool but also a medium for active learning and thinking. Classroom interaction refers to how teachers interact with students during whole class, group-based and one-to-one teaching. It is seen as a competence, termed by Walsh (2011) as "classroom interactional competence, which refers to teachers' and learners' ability to use interaction as a tool for mediating and assisting learning" (p. 158).

Classroom interaction has been widely accepted to underpin key domains of learning engagement. As defined by the Higher Education Academy[2] – a UK body responsible for the quality of learning and teaching in universities – and included in the UK Engagement Survey (www.heacademy.ac.uk), learning engagement includes such indicators as critical thinking, collaborative learning, staff-student interaction, reflecting on and connecting learning to real-world problems and issues, and creativity and communication skills development. Learning engagement has been shown to have a positive effect on student learning outcomes (Fritz, 2002; Hattie, 2011) as it fosters development of students' skills in thinking and writing (Bonwell & Sunderland, 1996; Neubauer, 2011; Zepke & Leach, 2010) and deep learning and learning autonomy (Gibbs & Coffey, 2004; Morgan, Martin, Howard, & Mihalek, 2005).

Positive links between learning engagement and outcomes are also supported by research into how the brain learns. Research with university students shows significant levels of retention and understanding being achieved through active approaches to learning that include discussion, learning by doing and teaching each other, compared to lecturing and demonstration, and individual student tasks such as reading (Sousa, 1995). This reflects the socio-cultural perspective "where learning is regarded as a social activity [...,] strongly influenced by [... active] engagement and participation" (Walsh, 2012, p. 1). Learning is especially

---

2. http://www.heaacademy.ac.uk/ research/surveys/united-kingdom-engagement-survey-ukes

enhanced when a student's current knowledge and understanding is scaffolded by an expert teacher (Larsen-Freeman, 2000; Vygotsky, 1962; Wells, 1999).

Despite the strength of theory and empirical research demonstrating the power of classroom discourse as a pedagogical tool and its critical role in improving the quality of the student learning experience, there is a widespread problem with student passivity and disengagement in the classroom, which is largely attributed to poor and restrictive tutor-student interaction (Hardman & Abd-Kadir, 2010; Herrmann, 2013; Rocca, 2010). Classroom discourse has been shown to be dominated by lengthy tutor monologues and recitations, characterised by short, quick-paced and closed question-answer sequences (Boyle, 2010; De Klerk, 1995, 1997; Hardman, 2015). Such teacher-led recitation often takes the prototypical form of a three-part exchange (Sinclair & Coulthard, 1992), consisting of an *initiation*, usually in the form of a tutor closed or recall question, a student *response,* which tends to be brief, and a *feedback* move, which is usually in the form of a low-level evaluation of the student's response, such as 'good' and 'well done'.

Such strict Initiation-Response-Feedback (IRF) teaching exchanges have been shown to place severe limitations on the contributions that students can make to the interaction and, hence, stifling their development of communicative competence (Garton, 2012; Nunan, 1987; Van Lier; 1996). It is "an unproductive interactional format' whereby students are "not provided opportunities for developing the complex interactional, linguistic and cognitive knowledge required in ordinary conversation" (Kasper, 2001, p. 518). The classroom discourse is controlled and dominated by the tutor at the expense of student active participation and less creative language use (Walsh, 2012).

It is recognised that there are numerous reasons for the pervasive use of the restrictive IRF teaching exchange. For example, there is a tendency by teachers to focus on the acquisition of knowledge as opposed to an acquisition of skills and attitudes, often reinforced by exam-oriented assessments (Bonwell & Sutherland, 1996). However in the case of language classrooms, open and high quality interaction is critical to how learners acquire a second language and operate as effective second language users. For example, as Macaro, Graham, and Woore (2016) argue, "pedagogy should be about developing language skills and therefore the teaching of linguistic knowledge (e.g. knowledge of grammar and vocabulary) should act in the service of skill development, not as an end in itself" (p. 5).

This paper stresses the critical role of classroom talk as a pedagogical tool and argues that tutors can be helped to enhance their classroom interactional competence and open-up classroom discourse so as to promote an active, collaborative and cognitively-engaging learning experience for their students.

2.   Opening-up classroom discourse

This paper largely draws on the concept of dialogic teaching (Alexander, 2008), which concerns itself with high quality teaching and learning talk. Dialogic teaching is based on a set of principles, which are as follows (Alexander, 2008, p. 28):

- *collective*: teachers and students address learning tasks together, whether as a group or as a class, rather than in isolation;

- *reciprocal*: teachers and students listen to each other, share ideas and consider alternative viewpoints;

- *supportive*: students articulate their ideas freely, without fear of embarrassment over 'wrong' answers; they help each other to reach common understandings;

- *cumulative*: teachers and students build on their own and each other's ideas and chain them into coherent lines of thinking and enquiry;

- *purposeful*: teachers plan and facilitate dialogic teaching with particular educational goals in view.

The emphasis of dialogic teaching on safe, open, jointly-constructed, cumulative and extended classroom discourse is also highlighted in the recent work of Macaro et al. (2016). They view high quality oral interaction as essential for language learning, where there should be substantial student turns – i.e. learners are encouraged to ask questions, to speak spontaneously and to say things without a fear of making mistakes – and appropriate feedback from tutors. This view in turn reflects two major second language acquisition theories, namely the Output Hypothesis that advocates spontaneous speech production in real communication (Swain, 1995), and the Interaction Hypothesis that supports the view that negotiation of meaning leads to better comprehension and facilitates language acquisition (Gass, Mackey, & Pica, 1998).

In other words, high quality classroom talk requires the loosening up of the tutor's control and breaking out of the limitations of the IRF recitation script through higher order questions and formative feedback strategies. Such question and feedback techniques are presented in Table 1 and Table 2 below, some of which are adapted from the work of Michaels and O'Connor (2012) on academically-productive talk in science teaching. Their feedback techniques are, to a great extent, deemed transferable to all subject disciplines.

It is proposed that tutors can open up the *initiation* move by including a balance of closed/narrow and open/authentic questions and encouraging student-initiated questions. Suggested question techniques and descriptions are presented in Table 1 below.

Table 1.   Question techniques and descriptions

Question techniques	Descriptions
Tutor closed questions	Tutor asks a closed question – allows one possible response
Tutor open question	Tutor asks an open question – allows various responses (e.g. What's your opinion?, 'What do you think?', 'How would you...?', How do you feel...?')
Student question	Student asks the tutor or another student a question

These question techniques can be used purposefully so as to generate and facilitate communication, encourage student participation, engage students with the teaching content, increase their understanding, develop thinking skills and help to formatively assess student learning.

It is also proposed that tutors can open up the *feedback* move so as to probe and build on students' contributions. Suggested feedback techniques and descriptions are presented in Table 2 below.

Table 2.   Feedback techniques and descriptions

Feedback techniques	Descriptions
Tutor acknowledge/ reject	Tutor accepts (or rejects) a student's contribution (e.g. nod, repeat answer, 'yes', 'ok', 'thank you', 'not quite the answer', 'incorrect')
Tutor praise	Tutor praises a student's contribution 'well done', 'good', 'brilliant'
Tutor comment	Tutor remarks, summarises, reformulates, builds on and/or transforms a student's contribution
Tutor redirect question	Tutor redirects the same (preceding) question to a different student
Tutor expand question	Tutor stays with the student and asks to say more (e.g. 'What do you mean by that?', 'Can you put that in another way?', 'Can you give an example?')
Tutor add-on question	Tutor asks students to add on to another student's contribution (e.g. 'Can anyone add on to ...?', 'Can anyone follow on from...?', 'Any comments on that?')
Tutor why question	Tutor stays with the same student and asks for evidence or reasoning (e.g. 'Why do you think that?', 'What is your evidence?')
Tutor revoice	Tutor verifies his/her understanding of a student's contribution (e.g. 'So, are you saying...?', 'Then I guess you think...')
Tutor agree-disagree question	Tutor asks if a student or students agree or disagree with another student's contribution (e.g. 'Do you agree/disagree and why?'), 'Does anyone want to respond to that?')
Tutor rephrase question	Tutor asks a student to repeat or reformulate his/her own or another student's contribution (e.g. 'Can you say it again?', 'Who can repeat what X just said in their own words?', 'What did your partner say?', 'Who can explain what X means when she says...?')
Tutor challenge question	Tutor provides a challenge or a counter-example (e.g. 'Does it always work that way?', 'What if...?', 'Is that always true?')

These feedback techniques can help to open up and extend classroom discourse, facilitate knowledge cumulation and a shared understanding, and encourage genuine communication and critical thinking. For example, tutor acknowledgement and praise are commonly used to create a supportive classroom. Tutor redirect, rephrase and add-on questions foster active listening and promote inclusivity and collaboration. Tutor 'why?', agree-disagree and challenge questions help to develop critical thinking.

3.   Classroom discourse analysis – illustration

The employment of some of the suggested question and feedback techniques is illustrated below in a transcript taken from a Teaching English to Speakers of Other Languages seminar attended by international students in the Education department of a UK university. This extract forms part of whole class teaching which directly follows student discussions in small groups.

Table 3.   Extract 1

1	T:	OK, I think we've had plenty of time to talk about it, so let's just see if we can get some kind of ideas about what is the value of the course book for students from your own experience as students?
2	S1:	I think they made the knowledge part more visible. You can look at the words (inaudible 00:20:46) pictures.
3	T:	What do you think? This is what you think, it makes the knowledge point more visible.
4	T:	Any comments on that? Can you see what Wendy is trying to say there?
5	SS:	[silence]
6	T:	Tell us more about this making it visible now, Wendy. In what way is it more visible?
7	S1:	Maybe when they listen to the part they don't quite know, maybe the material can make it more visible.
8	T:	Yes, Lin, go on...
9	S2:	Just like you give us a hand out, it helps us follow what you are saying.
10	T:	So that's the support, that's kind of what you are saying. It's good support to the teaching point
11	T:	Any others, good, any more?

Extract 1 presents a teaching exchange consisting of a stretch of turns, making good use of open questions and a range of types of feedback techniques. The exchange begins with an open question allowing for various responses from students and encouraging them to reflect on and connect to their real-life experiences. A fairly extended response, containing an explanation, is provided by a student (Wendy) in S.2. Rather than moving on immediately to a next student, the tutor stays with Wendy and tries to probe her further *'What do you think?'* in S.3. At the same time, he re-voices the student's response in order to verify his understanding of her contribution and to ensure that other students could hear and follow the discussion. Next, the tutor tries to open up and re-direct the discussion to other students, *'Any comments on that?'* in S.4. However, there is no student response (silence) to that open question in S.5.

The tutor does not close the discussion prematurely and instead returns to Wendy by asking her to elaborate on her previous contribution *'In what way is it more visible?'* in S.6. This is followed by a moderately detailed response from Wendy in S.7. This response seems to trigger a contribution from another student, which is highly encouraged by the tutor *'Yes, Lin, go on'* in S.8. Lin offers a comment *'Just like you give us a handout...'* in S. 9., which subsequently builds on Wendy's contribution. Lin's contribution is again followed by the tutor's re-voicing his understanding, *'that's kind of what you are saying'* in S.10. The tutor keeps the discussion going by inviting other students to contribute *'Any others...any more?'* and, simultaneously, praises the preceding students' contributions *'good'* in S.11. The praise is used as an important motivational strategy and, in combination with other feedback techniques, it reinforces the high value placed on dialogic teaching principles, resulting in high quality classroom talk.

4. Conclusion

Classroom discourse and interaction, if handled effectively and purposefully, can function as a very powerful pedagogical tool, fostering a safe, active, highly collaborative and cognitively stimulating learning experience for students.

There is a need to raise tutors' awareness of the critical role of classroom talk in teaching and learning and to enhance their classroom interactional competence. In particular, tutors should pay closer attention to their use of questions and feedback strategies and to make good use of a repertoire of these techniques that best suits their classroom context, such as in terms of class size, mixed ability group, teaching content and task types. There is also a need to make use of a balance of the teacher-centred recitations and learner-centred interactions. The latter would entail tutors' letting go of their dominance and tight control of the classroom discourse and empowering students to take charge of their own learning. Linked to this is a requirement for tutors to plan their teaching sessions carefully so as to create dialogic spaces where discussion and dialogues can purposefully take place to achieve particular educational goals.

Like tutors, students also need to develop their classroom interactional competence and become better interactants and learners. Therefore it is important for tutors to model to students effective classroom discourse practices and to provide them with ample opportunities to practise in class. This will also have a far reaching impact outside of the classroom in terms of students' transferable skills and learning autonomy.

5.   Acknowledgements

This paper is based on Jan Hardman's funded research project on classroom interaction patterns and dialogic teaching in university seminars across subject disciplines.

References

Alexander, R. (2008). *Towards dialogic teaching: rethinking classroom talk*. York: Dialogos.
Bonwell, C. C., & Sunderland, T. E. (1996). The active learning continuum: choosing activities to engage students in the classroom. *New Directions for Teaching and Learning, 67*, 3-16. http://dx.doi.org/10.1002/tl.37219966704

Boyle, A. (2010). *The dialogic construction of knowledge in university classroom talk. a corpus study of spoken academic discourse.* Unpublished PhD Thesis. Queen's University, Belfast.

De Klerk, V. (1995). Interaction patterns in post-graduate seminars: tutor versus student. *Language and Education, 9*(4), 249-64. http://dx.doi.org/10.1080/09500789509541418

De Klerk, V. (1997). Interaction patterns in university education. In B. Davies & D. Corson (Eds), *Encyclopaedia of language and education, Vol 3* (pp. 207-216). The Netherlands: Kluwer Academic Publishers. http://dx.doi.org/10.1007/978-94-011-4417-9_21

Fritz, M. (2002). Using learning styles inventories to promote active learning. *Journal of College reading and Learning, 32*(2), 183-188. http://dx.doi.org/10.1080/10790195.2002.10850297

Garton, S. (2012). Speaking out of turn? Taking the initiative in teacher-fronted classroom interaction. *Classroom Discourse, 3*(1), 29-45. http://dx.doi.org/10.1080/19463014.2012.666022

Gass, S., Mackey, A., & Pica, T. (1998). The role of input and interaction in second language acquisition: introduction to the special issue. *The Modern Language Journal, 83*(3), 299-307. http://dx.doi.org/10.1111/j.1540-4781.1998.tb01206.x

Gibbs, G., & Coffey, M. (2004). The impact of training of university teachers on their teaching skills, their approach to teaching and the approach to learning of their students. *Active Learning in Higher Education, 5*(1), 87-100. http://dx.doi.org/10.1177/1469787404040463

Hardman, J. (2015). Tutor-student interaction in seminar teaching: implications for professional development. *Active Learning in Higher Education, 17*(1), 1-14. http://dx.doi.org/10.1177/1469787415616728

Hardman, F., & Abd-Kadir, J. (2010). Classroom discourse: towards a dialogic pedagogy. In D. Wyse, R. Andrews & J. Hoffman (Eds), *The International Handbook of English, Language and Literacy* (pp. 254-264). London: Routledge.

Hattie, J. (2011). Visible Learning: synthesis of over 800 meta-analyses relating to achievement. London: Routledge.

Herrmann, K. J. (2013). The impact of cooperative learning on student engagement: results from an intervention. *Active Learning in Higher Education, 14*(3), 175-187. http://dx.doi.org/10.1177/1469787413498035

Kasper, G. (2001). Four perspectives on L2 pragmatic development. *Applied Linguistics, 22*(4), 502-530. http://dx.doi.org/10.1093/applin/22.4.502

Larsen-Freeman, D. (2000). Second language acquisition and applied linguistics. *Annual Review of Applied Linguistics, 20*, 165-181. http://dx.doi.org/10.1017/S026719050020010X

Macaro, E., Graham, S., & Woore, R. (2016). *Improving foreign langauge teaching: towards a research-based curriculum and pedagogy*. New York: Routledge.

Michaels, S., & O'Connor, C. (2012). *Talk science primer.* Cambridge, Massachussets: TERC.

Morgan, S., Martin, L., Howard B., & Mihalek, P. H. (2005). Active learning: what is it and why should I use it? *Developments in Business Simulation and Experiential Learning, 32*, 219-223.

Neubauer, D. (Ed.). (2011). *The emergent knowledge society and the future of higher education: Asian perspectives*. London: Routledge.

Nunan, D. (1987). Communicative language teaching: making it work. *ELT Journal, 12*(2), 136-145. http://dx.doi.org/10.1093/elt/41.2.136

Rocca, K. A. (2010). Student participation in the college classroom: an extended multidisciplinary literature review. *Communication Education, 59*(2), 185-312. http://dx.doi.org/10.1080/03634520903505936

Sinclair, J., & Coulthard, M. (1992). Towards an anlysis of discourse. In M. Coulthard (Ed.), *Advances in Spoken Discourse Analysis* (pp. 1-34). London: Routledge.

Sousa, D. (1995). *How the brain learns.* Roslon, V.A.: The National Association of Secondary School Principals.

Swain, M. (1995). Three functions of output in second language leanring. In G. Cook & B. Seidlhofer (Eds.), *Principles and Practice in Applied Linguistics* (pp. 125-144). Oxford: Oxford University Press.

Van Lier, L. (1996). *Interaction in the classroom: awareness, autonomy, and authenticity.* London: Longman.

Vygotsky, L. S. (1962). *Thought and language*. Cambridge, MA: MIT Press. http://dx.doi.org/10.1037/11193-000

Walsh, S. (2011). *Exploring classroom discourse: language in action*. London: Routledge.

Walsh, S. (2012). Conceptualising classroom interactional competence. *Novitas Royal: Research on Yourth and Language, 6*(1), 1-14.

Wells, G. (1999). *Dialogic inquiry: towards a sociocultural practice and theory of education*. Cambridge: Cambridge University Press. http://dx.doi.org/10.1017/CBO9780511605895

Zepke, N., & Leach, L. (2010). Improving student engagement: ten proposals for action. *Active Learning in Higher Education, 11*(3): 167-177, http://dx.doi.org/10.1177/1469787410379680

Section 1.

Fostering online collaboration

3 Evaluating the effects of a 'student buddy' initiative on student engagement and motivation

Anna Motzo[1]

Abstract

Motivation is one of the most important factors which influences second language learning (Dörnyei, 1998; Gardner & Lambert, 1972). A support mechanism which reinforces student motivation through encouragement, social interaction, feedback, sound learning environments and good teaching is crucial for ensuring successful learning. This is particularly relevant in distance or online language learning settings, as learners work more autonomously and independently than in conventional classrooms and there is a higher risk of feeling isolated and not part of a well-defined and supportive learning community. This paper presents initial research conducted by the Department of Languages at the Open University to evaluate the efficacy of a peer-support initiative on level 1 modules where the drop-out rate is significant. The study is supported by both qualitative and quantitative evidence, which evaluates student engagement on the forum, the support mechanisms offered by elected peers and their role in building an online community.

Keywords: peer support, online community, student engagement, motivation, distance learning.

1. The Open University, Milton Keynes, United Kingdom; a.motzo@open.ac.uk

How to cite this chapter: Motzo, A. (2016). Evaluating the effects of a 'student buddy' initiative on student engagement and motivation. In C. Goria, O. Speicher, & S. Stollhans (Eds), *Innovative language teaching and learning at university: enhancing participation and collaboration* (pp. 19-28). Dublin: Research-publishing.net. http://dx.doi.org/10.14705/rpnet.2016.000401

1. Introduction

In the last decade we have witnessed a substantial increase in distance/online language courses enhanced by the use of technology. Learners who choose to study at a distance use electronic devices such as computers, tablets or mobile phones to access materials and take part in both synchronous and asynchronous learning activities. This learning model is suited to the needs of students who have to combine professional, family and academic roles as it provides a high degree of learning flexibility. Motivation is identified as one of the most influential factors in student satisfaction and attainment and current research suggests that distance learners are more intrinsically motivated, self-confident and self-directed than on campus students (Rovai, Ponton, Wighting, & Baker, 2007). However, research also shows that distance institutions face a significantly higher problem with student retention and that the drop-out rates are between 10 to 20 percent higher than in traditional settings (Carr, 2000). In other words, even though institutions are able to attract learners to distance programmes, they are not always able to retain them.

2. The context

The Open University (OU) is the largest UK based distance university. Language courses are modular and are based on an opt-in (rather than opt-out) system. In other words, students do not enrol on a programme *ab initio*, instead they choose a number of modules, the completion of which will lead to a particular qualification. (Coleman & Furnborough, 2010).

Although students are expected to study independently and autonomously and the in-house created course materials reflect and enhance this approach, there are also well structured support mechanisms: all students enrolled on a module are assigned to a tutor and join a tutor group of a maximum of twenty students; they can attend optional synchronous face to face and online sessions (delivered via a teleconference system) as well as participate in asynchronous communication via the tutor group forum. In addition, students can connect with the wider module community via a (module) student forum, moderated by the module team.

In order to complete the module, students need to pass a certain number of written and spoken assignments as well as an 'end-of-module' exam. As might be expected, the attrition rate increases around assignment deadlines. This may be related to the main challenges faced by adult distance language learners such as:

- lack of opportunities to practise with others and share experiences;

- sense of isolation;

- increasing lack of confidence and motivation as the module progresses;

- perceived lack of informal 'outside the classroom' peer/social interaction.

3.   The 'student buddy' initiative

In an attempt to improve student retention and indirectly address the above mentioned challenges, in 2013, the OU's Department of Languages employed student buddies in *Intermediate* language modules to offer peer support via a designated forum thread prior to assignment deadlines. Following the pilot, in the academic year 2014-15, the initiative was extended to all level 1 language modules with the employment of one or two 'student buddies', depending on the module population.

The rationale of the initiative was:

- to offer students a friendly and supportive platform (through a dedicated thread in the student forum) for two weeks prior to each assignment deadline;

- to encourage learners through the presence of the student buddy to informally connect with peers and share ideas about how to tackle assignments;

- to help learners to maintain motivation as well as boost each other's confidence through mutual encouragement.

The buddies were former students who:

- had recently completed the module;

- were able to demonstrate a high degree of familiarity with the course materials;

- were competent users of IT tools;

- had excellent communication skills.

Buddies were recruited by the module chairs and received synchronous group online training. They were also supported throughout the year by the module chair through on-going feedback. Buddies were also able to support each other via their own web space and 'buddy forum'. They were expected to open a *sticky thread*[2] two weeks prior to each assignment and to check the thread at least once a day. They were required to send motivational messages, which included study tips, practical advice on where to find details on assignment tasks and to send reminders of completion dates and generally encouraging postings. An overview of the different student buddy-led threads indicates that the personal style adopted by the buddy in order to provide support was crucial to ensure the formation and development of an online community. Where the buddy's style tended to be more friendly and open, student engagement and participation was more active.

---

2. In the education software Moodle, the sticky discussion option can be used to pin a thread so that the pinned thread stays on the top of the list, even after newer discussions are posted.

An in-depth evaluation of whether the student buddy initiative on level 1 Language modules had a positive impact on student retention lies beyond the scope of this contribution and will be carried out elsewhere. The purpose of this paper is to present initial findings of the buddy initiative gathered from the *beginners'* modules and to evaluate whether it had a positive impact on increasing informal social cohesion.

4. Data collection and analysis

The study is based on a range of data collection methods such as student survey results, the analysis of one student forum (beginners' French), as well as in-depth interviews with both buddies and students, as shown in Figure 1.

Figure 1.   Data collection

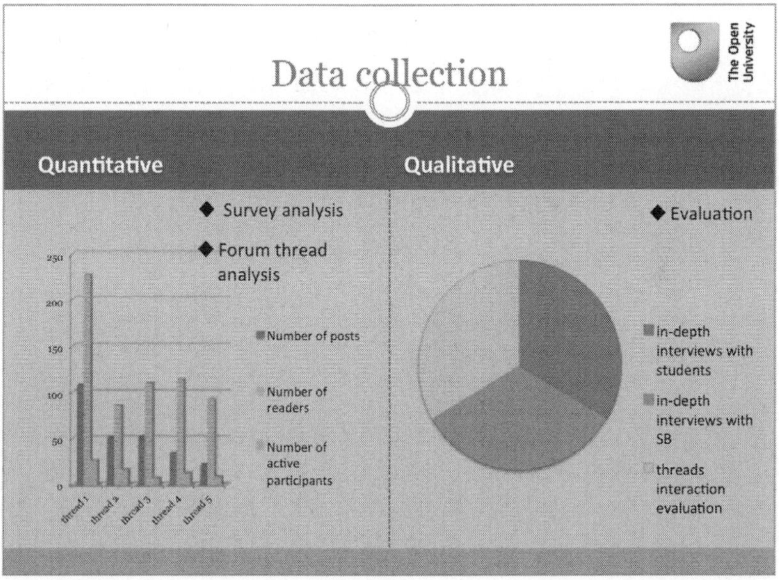

Initial findings from the all the *beginners'* surveys indicate that students highly valued the initiative, 92% and 82% respectively of the sample thought it was good to have a student buddy and that it was helpful for moral support and reassurance and a substantial majority found it useful to clarify assignment requirements (64%) and that it was helpful in engendering a feeling of not being alone (66%).

The initial research also confirms the important role played by the buddy in building a sense of community.

Quotes from students:

"It puts a **personal face on the course** and helps students who want to get course **advice from a "friend"** yet at the same time, know that they are working in your best interest (where a real friend might accidently push you in the wrong direction)".

"**Those wanting support and feeling isolated** could find it useful".

"**Might feel less alone** with the studying".

"It may be **useful for people who have little contact with others** on their module, or those who are particularly nervous or stressed".

"It provides extra help and **companionship** for the student".

A close up of the beginners' French forum threads suggests four waves of student engagement:

I. Student buddy to whole group: student buddy sends general information, reminders of deadlines and general motivational messages as per briefing. Engenders a friendly atmosphere.

II. Student to student buddy: student asks practical and experiential questions, seeks feedback on his/her own approach and seeks general reassurance.

III. Student buddy to student: answers queries, provides *ad hoc* moral and practical support, boosts confidence, shares his/her own tacit knowledge.

IV. Student(s) to student(s): respond to practical questions; boost each other's confidence and motivation, share ideas, feelings and build friendship.

It needs to be noted that not all the above mentioned elements were present from the beginning, on the contrary, a careful study of the threads shows a progressive transition from general, formal rather factual postings – mainly initiated by the student buddy – to more informal, colloquial and even spontaneous postings generated by all participants. As the time progressed, the participants in the thread became closer to each other and more open to sharing personal feelings related to the module (such as showing anxiety, sharing a sense of achievement and providing encouragement to others).

Participants were also keen to share personal anecdotes which exceeded the module-content (such as talking about the birth of a grand-daughter or the death of a dog, or the approaching holidays). It is also noteworthy that as the atmosphere became more friendly and colloquial, a number of peripheral participants, who hitherto had only read the forum without posting anything, progressively made the transition to become active participants, able and happy to share their views with others.

As the module progressed, signs that an online community had formed were also found. Evidence that participants mattered to each other (McMillan & Chavis, 1986), kept together in the pursuit of common goals (Westheimer & Kahne, 1993), and felt interdependent (Bellah et al., 1985) while developing a sense of friendship, bonding and trust, was also identified in the textual analysis. As the language used by the participants became more idiomatic, full of colloquialisms and more expressive with an increasing use of emoticons and symbols replacing words (Figure 2), the style adopted by the users mirrored that of informal social networks.

Figure 2.   Textual analysis

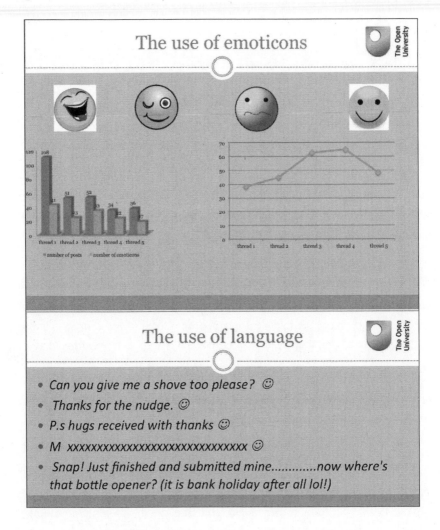

5.   Conclusion

When it comes to distance education, historically, too much emphasis has been placed on learner independence and autonomy and not enough on interdependence and social presence. The student buddy scheme has been introduced to OU level 1 language modules as a retention initiative with the aim to provide students with peer support at crucial times. Conversely, a close analysis of the impact of this initiative on student engagement and motivation found that the presence of the buddy played a crucial role in enhancing social presence and team building with some positive effects on student satisfaction and persistence.

6.   Acknowledgements

The author would like to thank the following people:

- Professor Jim Coleman (The Open University, UK) for his support and insightful guidance during this study.

- The Student Buddies Scholarship project team members at the Department of Languages, The Open University: Nel Boswood, Jo Fayram, Tim Jilg, Anna Proudfoot and Kan Qian.

References

Bellah, R. N., Madsen, R., Sullivan, W. M., Swidler, A., & Tipton, S. M. (1985). *Habits of the heart*. Berkeley: University of California Press.

Carr, S. (2000). As distance education comes of age, the challenge is keeping the students. *The Chronicle of Higher Education, 46*(23), A39-A41.

Coleman, J. A., & Furnborough, C. (2010). Learner characteristics and learning outcomes on a distance Spanish course for beginners. *System, 38*(1), 14-29. http://dx.doi.org/10.1016/j.system.2009.12.002

Dörnyei, Z. (1998). Motivation in second and foreign language learning. *Language Teaching, 31*(3), 117-135. http://dx.doi.org/10.1017/S026144480001315X

Gardner , R. C., & Lambert, W. E. (1972). Attitudes and motivation in second language learning. Rowley, MA: Newbury House.

McMillan, D. W., & Chavis, D. M. (1986). Sense of community: a definition and theory. *Journal of Community Psychology, 14*(1), 6-23.

Rovai, A. P., Ponton, M. K., Wighting, M. J., Baker, J. D. (2007). A comparative analysis of student motivation in traditional classroom and e-learning. *International Journal on E-Learning, 6*(3), 413-432.

Westheimer, J., & Kahne, J. (1993). Building school communities: an experience-based model. Phi Delta Kappan, 75(4), 324-28.

4 "Show me where you study!" – An interactive project between German language students in Nottingham and St Andrews

Insa Hartung[1] and Sandra Reisenleutner[2]

Abstract

Interactive projects among students of a Common European Framework of Reference for languages (CEFR) A1+/A2 level seem difficult to set up due to the limited language repertoire of the students. Thus, our aim was to take up the challenge and start a project with the objective of applying their language skills. We chose a collaborative approach to this project in order to offer students a shared learning experience.

Keywords: cross-university collaboration, CEFR A2 language courses, *VoiceThread*, university town, projects within the CEFR.

1.   Introduction

Cross-university projects for language students at an elementary level can prove challenging due to the limited language repertoire, and they are, therefore, not very widespread. The project "Show me where you study!" seeks to take up this challenge and presents an innovative approach to enhance collaboration in German language teaching. Designed for students at the CEFR level A1+/A2, the project was run during the academic session 2014/15 at the University of Nottingham and the University of St Andrews.

1. University of St Andrews, St Andrews, United Kingdom; ih30@st-andrews.ac.uk

2. University of Nottingham, Nottingham, United Kingdom; Sandra.Reisenleutner@nottingham.ac.uk

How to cite this chapter: Hartung, I., & Reisenleutner, S. (2016). "Show me where you study!" – An interactive project between German language students in Nottingham and St Andrews. In C. Goria, O. Speicher, & S. Stollhans (Eds), *Innovative language teaching and learning at university: enhancing participation and collaboration* (pp. 29-36). Dublin: Research-publishing.net. http://dx.doi.org/10.14705/rpnet.2016.000402

2.   Setting

The project was carried out in two undergraduate student groups enrolled at the universities of Nottingham and St Andrews in March 2015. In Nottingham, the group consisted of Stage 2 language students of the Language Centre. In St Andrews, the students were in the second semester of the so-called "beginners' course" at the German department. Both courses were at an A2 level.

The topics that had been covered before the project started included tourism, holiday and leisure. Within these topics, and by using an action-oriented approach, students had previously learnt to:

- plan a holiday;

- engage in a conversation talking about holidays and holiday destinations;

- make enquiries;

- read information in travel guide books.

Taking this context as a starting point, the idea arose to run a project in which students created their own travel guide book about their university town. The title was "Show me where you study" and involved student exchanges via the digital tool *VoiceThread*.

Students were required to work in groups and research various aspects (see below). In order to add a ludic aspect to the project, students had to guess the other town and thus, were not allowed to mention the name of their own university.

The topic areas were local food, university and university life, leisure time and night life, as well as surrounding areas.

3.   General objectives

Among our objectives was the enhancement of collaborative and cooperative learning in CEFR A2 German language courses. Collaboration and cooperation are often used interchangeably as the concepts feature the same criteria: symmetry, common goals, and division of labour among group members (Dillenbourg, 1999, p. 8). However, Dillenbourg (1999) argues: "[i]n cooperation, partners split the work, solve sub-tasks individually and then assemble the partial results into the final output. In collaboration, partners do the work 'together'" (p. 8). This means there is only a minimal division of labour.

We are aware that our project contains both collaborative and cooperative aspects. On the one hand, the project has a tangible end product which is an indicator for collaboration, while the contributions of each group remain very much visible, which suggests cooperative learning.

In addition, it was important for us to move beyond common group work and provide students with more than a mere exchange of facts and recommendations, which meant moving beyond a simple "hook-up" and "exchange of information", and to attempt to foster team work in a learning project (Dooly, 2008, p. 66). More precisely, Dooly (2008) recommends that "students' interaction must be linked to the others in such a way that the success of the planned activity can be achieved only by everyone contributing their part" (p. 72).

In particular, the project focuses on reflecting the use of language in a "real-life" situations and offers the opportunity to apply previously acquired language skills and knowledge. Hence, the approach was action-orientated. By creating something themselves at the end of a learning unit, it was our aim to raise students' awareness of how much they had achieved and what they are able to create at this language level.

For the wider course curriculum, we wanted to create multiple benefits such as fostering team-work skills, researching a topic and working with a new digital tool.

4.   Language specific objectives

In addition to the general objectives, it was fundamental that the focus remained on the use of language. Thus, by analysing the material we had worked with, we identified the following categories the students were required to include (see Table 1).

Table 1.   Language specific objectives

Vocabulary	Grammar	Structures	Style	Functions
holiday tourism	adjective endings	relative clauses (St Andrews)	guide book	addressing people
leisure time activities	reflexive verbs	subordinate clauses	positive describing	commenting and guessing
	comparative superlative			asking questions

This table, for the most part, reflects the language descriptors of the CEFR (Council of Europe, 2001) and *Profile Deutsch* at A2 level which are a good reference for setting learning outcomes.

5.   Project stages

The project consisted of five stages which will be described in the following.

5.1.   Introduction to the project and the e-tool *VoiceThread*

In class, we introduced the project to our students and explained the use of the e-tool *VoiceThread*. Students also chose their topic areas and received instructions about the language requirements and the design of the tourist guide.

5.2. Topic research and writing in groups

In groups, students researched their topics and wrote their contribution in a Word-document, where they also included pictures. The text length was around 250 words. This stage was carried out in a different way in St Andrews and in Nottingham: Nottingham used more class-time whereas students in St Andrews had to research and write as part of their homework.

5.3. Text and picture upload

The initial idea was for students to upload their own contributions on *VoiceThread*. However, due to time constraints and for practical reasons, students sent their projects via e-mail to the teachers, who uploaded it and made it accessible to the other group.

5.4. Read contributions and comment

After receiving the other group's guide book, students had to read through it and make one written and one audio comment on *VoiceThread*. For instance, they could ask questions, comment on the pictures and/or text (e.g. "This looks nice."/ "What is the weather like?"/ "This club looks better than the ones here.") and try to guess the place.

5.5. Response to the comments received

In the last stage of the project, students were asked to refer back to the comments and questions received. These final comments presented the official end of the project.

In this context, it is also important to mention the preparatory work that had to be carried out by the teachers before starting the project. In order to ensure that the project ran smoothly, good communication and collaboration was indispensable. By using *Dropbox*, e-mail and *Skype*, ideas were exchanged, project outlines drafted, learning aims set and a time plan created. Furthermore, the use of *VoiceThread* was discussed and prepared (i.e. signing up students, testing different functions).

6. Results and further discussion

A graphic analysis of the project on the comment frequency is presented in Figure 1. With a total number of 22 students (13 in Nottingham and 9 in St Andrews), the groups were well balanced. The results clearly indicate a strong preference for written comments (n=44) in comparison to audio comments (n=13). This thought-provoking result was not what had been expected, as we assumed the out-of-class use would encourage students to make more audio comments.

Figure 1.   Students' comment frequency

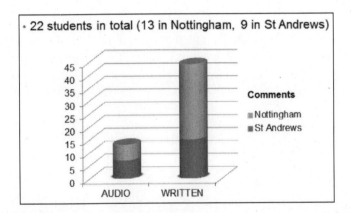

The feedback for the project was very positive and demonstrated that students liked working in teams and enjoyed applying their language skills. However, for future projects of this kind there are a few aspects to consider that we would like to discuss in this section.

One interesting outcome was that students posted much fewer audio comments than written ones (see Figure 1). Thus, speaking might not necessarily be facilitated by placing it outside of the language classroom. The audio comment function on *VoiceThread* makes it possible for students to record themselves several times, listen to their audio file and make it accessible to others whenever they decide. This is clearly one of the positive aspects as it enables learners to listen to their own pronunciation and work on it. However, the fact of publishing an audio comment so that it can be heard by others (again and again – on the contrary to classroom contributions) does not put all students at ease.

Whatever digital tool is used for such a project (a free alternative is *Dropbox*), it is fundamental to be aware of the limitations it might have. For some tools, licenses are required, while others are freely accessible, but might be problematic in terms of data protection. It is essential to keep in mind that students need to have access to the technical facilities in order to use the tool and participate in the project.

The question remains open as to how the project could be assessed. As MacKinnon (2013) points out in her Higher Education Academy report, "using e-tools to facilitate international collaborations and enhance language teaching" could lead to a "lack of assessment or reward for engagement" which then "can significantly reduce participation as students are very strategic in the use of their time" (p. 22). Although we did not assess the project and did not give any reward, students were informed about learning outcomes and the benefits of participating in the project. In this project, producing a small guide-book and seeing the result might be a reward in itself.

A similar challenge was how to deal with mistakes as students' contributions were done in team-work and shared within the groups. In this case, we used some descriptors of the CEFR as a reference and focused on the communicative ability rather than on correcting every mistake. Especially when work is published and shared with other groups, teachers might feel the need to correct everything.

However, we refrained from this in order to encourage students to participate more. Only mistakes made in their presentations were pointed out if they were regarded as very important.

To summarise, we would like to repeat a similar project as the advantages prevailed. However, aspects like assessment, rewards and how to deal with mistakes still need more reflection to ensure that students are motivated, enjoy participating and at the same time apply and improve their language skills.

References

Council of Europe (2001). *Common European framework of reference for languages: learning, teaching, assessment.* Cambridge: Cambridge University Press.

Dillenbourg, P. (1999). What do you mean by 'collaborative learning'? In P. Dillenbourg (Ed.), *Collaborative learning: cognitive and computational approaches* (pp. 1-19). Oxford, UK: Elsevier.

Dooly, M. (2008). Understanding the many steps for effective collaborative language projects. *The Language Learning Journal, 36*(1), 65-78.

MacKinnon, T. (2013). *Using e-tools to facilitate international collaborations and enhance language teaching.* The Higher Education Academy. Retrieved from http://www.ucml. ac.uk/sites/default/files/pages/160/Using_e_tools.pdf

5 TANGO, an international collaborative bilingual e-learning project

Carmen Álvarez-Mayo[1]

Abstract

TANGO (Álvarez-Mayo, 2013) uses the cultural aspects of foreign languages to promote oral interaction, enabling students to become self-regulated learners. Through TANGO, foreign language students learn about the cultural intricacies of the Target Language (TL) and use the TL to practise and further develop their oral skills with a partner who is a native speaker. Students openly discuss their views and reflect on their learning progress and any issues they may encounter while practising all language skills: listening, reading, writing and oral interaction. TANGO is an e-learning programme that promotes self-regulated learning as well as critical thinking and as such it will play a key role in making foreign language students better equipped learners, enabling them to develop invaluable continual development skills for their academic and professional careers.

Keywords: intercultural communicative competence, e-learning, collaborative work, autonomous learning, critical thinking.

1.   Introduction: topics and tasks

As already discussed in Álvarez-Mayo (2015b), TANGO consists of two bilingual websites. One site hosts the Spanish and English tasks, and the other is the e-portfolio (see also Álvarez-Mayo, 2015a) where the pilot students

1. University of York, United Kingdom; carmen.alvarez-mayo@york.ac.uk

How to cite this chapter: Álvarez-Mayo, C. (2016). TANGO, an international collaborative bilingual e-learning project. In C. Goria, O. Speicher, & S. Stollhans (Eds), *Innovative language teaching and learning at university: enhancing participation and collaboration* (pp. 37-48). Dublin: Research-publishing.net. http://dx.doi.org/10.14705/rpnet.2016.000403

published their work. Tasks in both languages are akin, as they have been planned around the same grammatical and cultural topics relevant to the course outline. They have been purposely developed to help students reflect on similarities and differences between both languages and cultures in order to promote intercultural competence (Deardorff, 2004). Tasks have been designed following a communicative approach and are influenced by Critical Pedagogy (Breunig, 2011), encouraging critical thinking to develop socially active individuals.

When I devised TANGO I wanted to create authentic tasks: real, varied and motivating tasks which would be different every time and for every learner; that could be approached as a whole or broken into individual parts, as illustrated in Figure 1.

Figure 1.   D. English regions

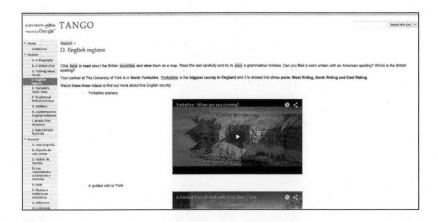

Being a collaborative project (Center for Teaching and Learning, 1999), I wanted to ensure that all students would play a key role. Therefore, all activities were designed with the students at the core, revolving around the students' experience and interests, i.e. culture, food, traditions, geography, hobbies, music, film, and literature. Sharing their own knowledge and experiences, real and meaningful discussions would develop, and genuine communication and reflection would be generated and would increase the students' understanding of one another and the TL they are studying:

"A DMC [Directed Motivational Current] is recognisable when the journey toward a goal does not merely consist of conscientious, concentrated hard work, but instead exhibits signs of something more—a serendipitous coming-together of circumstances and conditions—leading the project to take on a life of its own and stream past initial expectations to a point way out in the distance" (Dörnyei, Henry, & Muir, in press, p. xii).

2.   Aims of the project

The University of York Languages For All (LFA) Programme provides a formal basis in the development of the four key language skills: speaking, listening, reading and writing. However due to time constraints, few extension activities to develop cultural awareness can be provided, see Figure 2.

TANGO was devised to enhance the students' learning experience, bringing foreign language learners the opportunity to practise the TL with a native speaker in order to help them cultivate oral interaction skills.

Figure 2.   D. Las comunidades autónomas y Asturias ('The autonomous counties and Asturias')

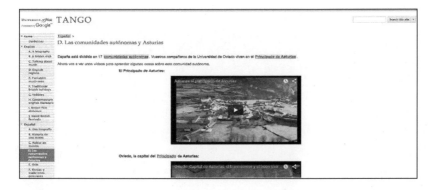

This new language program was piloted with post-beginner students from the University of York (UoY) and English intermediate students from the University of Oviedo (UoO). At the start of the 2013/14 academic year, the UoY Spanish students had a CEFR A1 level of proficiency (Council of Europe, 2001), similar to a General Certificate of Secondary Education (GCSE) in the British education system. By the end of the academic year the UoY Spanish learners who had actively participated in the pilot achieved an A2/B1 in the CEFR, similar to an A-Level in the United Kingdom.

The feedback received from the participants in the pilot of TANGO reflected that the students found the project very beneficial as they had experienced a remarkable improvement in their language skills. Students became acquainted and familiar with cultural concepts and their confidence using the TL improved substantially. They developed a deeper language awareness not yet achieved by many upper-intermediate foreign language students, and consequently they became intermediate level students.

As noted in their feedback, students became more confident learners while they practised and developed valuable skills needed to complete the project's tasks, such as reading and researching topics to be able to discuss their findings with their partners and share their views and experiences. They also wrote and published the fortnightly essays in their individual online portfolios (Veenman, Van Hout-Wolters, & Afflerbach, 2006) and reflecting on their learning provided feedback and help to one another.

Students worked in a professional manner and acquired transferable skills to help them become autonomous learners: they worked independently and in small teams, were fully in charge of their work, research and practice; organised and agreed their work schedules; used a variety of documents; researched topics individually and in collaboration with their partners; discussed their ideas and experiences in both languages and were creative presenting their findings and writing their essays. While doing all that, students used and developed IT skills to publish and share their work; behaved professionally, exercising respect and understanding with one another and became more aware of diversity, see

Figure 3. The students who participated in TANGO practised 'self-regulated learning': "learning that occurs largely from the influence of students' self-generated thoughts, feelings, strategies, and behaviors, which are oriented toward the attainment of goals" (Schunk & Zimmerman, 1998, p. viii).

Figure 3.   C. Talking about music: sample of an English student portfolio (1)

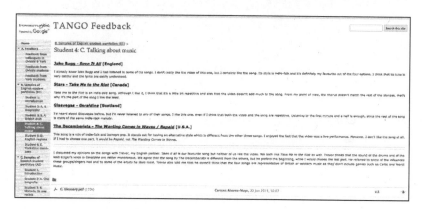

During the project, students reflected on their learning through "new eyes" (Proust, 1923, p. 237), and developed what Michael Byram (1997) refers to as 'intercultural communicative competence'. They practised 'critical cultural awareness': the ability "to question, to analyse, to evaluate and, potentially, to take action" (Byram, 2008, p. 146). Furthermore, based in Kolb's (1984) Experimental Learning Cycle, TANGO has provided a safe environment to practise and develop Deardorff's (2006) Process Model of Intercultural Competence, "a continuous process of working on attitudes, knowledge, internal outcomes and external outcomes related to intercultural competence" (Moeller & Nugent, 2014, p. 4).

Students had the opportunity to learn new vocabulary and idiomatic expressions (Figure 4), while practising and further developing their command of the TL in the four main language skills as well as exercising real communication and genuine oral interaction, utilising and acquiring the relevant skills to successfully communicate and interact in the TL.

Figure 4. C. Talking about music: sample of an English student portfolio (2)

TANGO (Week 6)

C. TALKING ABOUT MUSIC

GLOSSARY

Word	Spanish translation	Definition	Example
Anoint *(Verb)*	Ungir	To put oil or water on somebody's head as part of a religious ceremony.	The priest anointed her with oil.
Cradle *(Noun)*	Cuna	A small bed for a baby which can be pushed gently from side to side.	The baby was sleeping in its cradle.
Despise *(Verb)*	Despreciar / Menospreciar	To dislike and have no respect for somebody/something.	You shouldn't despise her for what she did.
Glen *(Noun)*	Cañada / Valle	A deep narrow valley, especially in Scotland or Ireland.	It was located near a Scottish glen.
Nickel *(Noun)*	Moneda de cinco centavos	A coin of the US and Canada worth 5 cents.	I need another nickel for the parking meter.
Ore *(Noun)*	Mineral	Rock, earth, etc. from which metal can be obtained.	That mine has a reserve of ore.
Pall *(Noun)*	Nube	A thick dark cloud of something.	The pall covered all they could see.
Reedy *(Adjective)*	Lleno de juncos.	Full of reeds.	We walked near a reedy river.
Shepherd *(Noun)*	Pastor	A person whose job is to take care of sheep.	A shepherd must take care of his sheep.
To turn the tide *(Idiom)*	Cambiar el curso	Reverse the trend of events.	This is the last chance for us to turn the tide of our future.
Wayward *(Adjective)*	Caprichoso / Obstinado	Difficult to control.	His wayward behaviour is going to bring him problems.
Window ledge *(Noun)*	Alféizar	A narrow shelf below a window, either inside or outside.	He put a plant on the window ledge of his office.

3. Collaboration and human e-motion

In the 21st century, technology is fundamental in communication to foster relationships, both personal and professional, and to share knowledge, experiences and opinions. Depending on our personality, our history and personal experience, some of us find it easier than others to establish relationships; perceptions, attitudes and beliefs play an important role in this too. Consequently, establishing a good relationship amongst peers is crucial to develop highly effective teams (Balsom, Barrass, Michela, & Zdaniuk, 2009) and achieve success in a collaborative endeavour (Figure 5).

Figure 5.   TANGO homepage

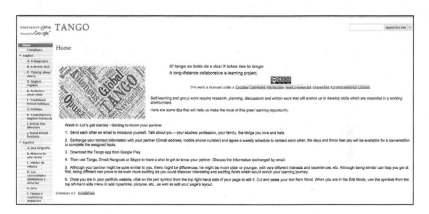

Setting firm foundations and sharing general safe guarding information to ensure that students were respectful with one another was essential for the success of the project. After some initial research (Jones, 2008; Neville, 2009; Working Group on QA for Distance Learning, 2013) and reflection, guidelines were devised for students to create a safe environment where experiences and views could be shared in a respectful and professional manner. These guidelines were published on both TANGO websites, see Figure 6.

Throughout the pilot of TANGO, students used technology to a more extensive level than it is normally incorporated into the teaching and learning process. They relied on Skype and Google Hangouts to communicate synchronously, to discuss each task, the notes they took, their experiences, ideas and opinions. They openly discussed tasks and received feedback from one another before and after publishing work in the e-portfolios.

The Internet has given us the opportunity to discover and share ideas and knowledge. Using the online space each student was allocated, they became authors and publishers, and were creative and original in developing their own styles. They appreciated and valued their own effort and acquired a better understanding of the TL and culture as well as their own. Our cultures are varied, complex and multifaceted; it is important that learners become more aware of diversity: culturally, regionally, locally, so that they can increasingly become more understanding and respectful with one another, not only internationally but at every level.

Figure 6.   TANGO guidelines

Openly discussing and sharing our experiences enable us to reflect and learn from them and with each other. TANGO and the e-portfolios use the Internet, communication tools and apps currently available to bring together students not only from different countries, but from a variety of cultures, backgrounds and ages.

4.   Conclusion

Tutors and students in Oviedo and York provided very positive feedback on materials, methodology and impact.

The students' learning experience was enriched by a deepening of cultural knowledge about aspects which they had previously not encountered. They noted improvement in a range of key skills such as writing, speaking and vocabulary acquisition and mentioned in their feedback that they found the pilot very useful and would like to participate in TANGO again.

Essential workplace skills were practised and developed: time-management, working with others, document use, reading, oral communication, critical thinking and discussion, grammar, translation, writing, digital technology, and continual development skills.

There was a clear appreciation of individual contact with a native speaker and an in-depth sharing of experiences in pairs. Students shared their life experiences, real experiences within a real context and learnt about the cultural intricacies embedded in language learning.

Students reflected on their learning process, discussed issues they have experienced while doing their work and developed a better understanding of the target language due to the nature of the peer-mentoring partnership they fostered.

Independent learning was promoted and practised by students. Self-regulated learning was embedded in the project and participants were encouraged to work with flexibility and to organise their work and contact time, thus developing lifelong learning skills. Learners were guided and supported to take control of their own learning.

Students were led towards planning their own work, they were provided with forms to monitor their own progress after each completed task and they were requested to provide feedback reflecting on their work and learning experience. Ongoing discussion and reflection on the students' work and learning progress were promoted and practised throughout the project.

Each learner is an individual, and although we share many characteristics we have our very own distinctive traits which make us all unique. Some of us can remember facts and events particularly well, some can recall vividly what they see, others have a sensory memory and can remember experiences very clearly, including smells, tastes, temperature, etc., yet unconsciously, we all can remember what we regularly do and practise again and again in order to become better at something: playing an instrument, a sport, or, in this case, learning and using a foreign language. The more often we practise something, the better our understanding of the subject, the higher the standard we can achieve and deliver, and the more developed our implicit memory (Schacter, 1987) becomes (commonly referred to as 'muscle memory') – in the same way that our muscles improve with exercise when they are utilised.

References

Álvarez-Mayo, C. (2013). *TANGO (Themed Autonomous Navigation Global Opus)*. Retrieved from https://sites.google.com/a/york.ac.uk/tango/

Álvarez-Mayo, C. (2015a). *TANGO Feedback.*Retrieved from https://sites.google.com/a/york.ac.uk/tango-feedback/

Álvarez-Mayo, C. (2015b). TANGO (themed autonomous navigation global opus), a bilingual international collaborative e-learning project. *EDULEARN15 Proceedings* (pp. 272-281). Retrieved from http://library.iated.org/view/ALVAREZMAYO2015TAN

Balsom, M., Barrass, R., Michela, J., & Zdaniuk, A. (2009). Processes and attributes of highly effective teams. *The WORC Group, University of Waterloo*. Retrieved from https://uwaterloo.ca/psychology/sites/ca.psychology/files/uploads/files/processesattributeseffectiveteams.jm_.v4.pdf

Breunig, M. (2011). Problematazing critical pedagogy. *International Journal of Critical Pedagogy, 3*(3), 2-23.

Byram, M. (1997). *Teaching and assessing intercultural communicative competence.* UK: Multilingual Matters Ltd.

Byram, M. (2008). *From foreign language education to education for intercultural citizenship. Essays and reflections.* UK: Multilingual Matters Ltd.

Council of Europe. (2001). *Common European framework of reference for languages: learning, teaching, assessment.* Retrieved from http://www.coe.int/t/dg4/linguistic/Cadre1_en.asp

Center for Teaching and Learning. (1999). Cooperative learning: students working in small groups. *Stanford University Newsletter on Teaching, 10*(2). Retrieved from http://web. stanford.edu/dept/CTL/Newsletter/cooperative.pdf

Deardorff, D. K. (2004). Internationalization: in search of intercultural competence. *International Educator, 13*(2), 13-15. Retrieved from http://www.nafsa.org/_/file/_/in_ search_of_intercultural.pdf

Deardorff, D. K. (2006). Identification and assessment of intercultural competence as a student outcome of internationalization. *Journal of Studies in International Education, 10*(3), 241-266. http://dx.doi.org/10.1177/1028315306287002

Dörnyei, Z., Henry, A., & Muir, C. (in press). *Motivational currents in language learning: frameworks for focused interventions.* New York: Routledge. Preface retrieved from http://www.zoltandornyei.co.uk/uploads/preface-16.pdf

Jones, K. (2008). Online work guidelines. *CEEBL (Centre for Excellence in Enquiry Based Learning).* The University of Manchester. Retrieved from http://www.ceebl.manchester. ac.uk/resources/guides/Online_Group_Work_Guidelines.pdf

Kolb, D. A. (1984). *Experimental Learning.* Englewood Cliffs, NJ: Prentice Hall.

Moeller, A. J., & Nugent, K. (2014). Building intercultural competence in the language classroom. In S. Dhonau (Ed.), *Unlock the gateway to communication, selected papers from the 2014 Central States conference on the teaching of foreign languages* (pp. 1-18). Richmond, VA: Robert M. Terry. Retrieved from http://www.csctfl.org/ documents/2014Report/CSCTFLReport2014.pdf

Neville, C. (2009). Making groupwork work. *Learn higher CETL.* The University of Bradford. Retrieved from http://new.learnhigher.ac.uk/blog/wp-content/uploads/ groupwork-booklet.pdf

Proust, M. (1923). *In Search of Lost Time, Vol. V: The Prisoner.* Penguin Modern Classics 2003 edition.

Schacter, D. L. (1987). Implicit memory: history and current status. *Journal of Experimental Psychology: Learning, Memory and Cognition, 13*(3), 501-518. http://dx.doi. org/10.1037/0278-7393.13.3.501

Schunk, D. H., & Zimmerman, B. J. (1998). *Self-regulated learning: from teaching to self-reflective practice.* New York, NY: Guilford Press.

Veenman, M., Van Hout-Wolters, B., & Afflerbach, P. (2006). Metacognition and learning: conceptual and methodological considerations. *Metacognition Learning, 1*(1), 3-14. http://dx.doi.org/10.1007/s11409-006-6893-0

Working Group on QA for Distance Learning. (2013). *Quality framework for distance learning programmes*. University of York. Retrieved from https://vle.york.ac.uk/bbcswcbdav/institution/Distance%20Learning%20Forum/Quality%20Framework%20Website/DLF_Home.html

6 Open and anonymous peer review in a digital online environment compared in academic writing context

Salim Razı[1]

Abstract

This study compares the impact of 'open' and 'anonymous' peer feedback as an adjunct to teacher-mediated feedback in a digital online environment utilising data gathered on an academic writing course at a Turkish university. Students were divided into two groups with similar writing proficiencies. Students peer reviewed papers either anonymously or openly, then resubmitted them. The lecturer provided feedback and students again resubmitted their assignments. Finally, students submitted a reflection paper on how or whether they benefited from both peer and teacher-mediated feedback. Findings provide evidence for the positive contribution of multiple anonymous peer feedback in a digital online environment towards improved academic writing skills.

Keywords: academic writing, anonymous peer review, digital peer review, English for academic purposes, EAP, plagiarism detectors.

1.   Introduction

Peer review may allow learners to overcome problems they encounter in Foreign Language (FL) learning since they receive assistance and feedback

1. Canakkale Onsekiz Mart University, Turkey; salimrazi@gmail.com

How to cite this chapter: Razı, S. (2016). Open and anonymous peer review in a digital online environment compared in academic writing context. In C. Goria, O. Speicher, & S. Stollhans (Eds), *Innovative language teaching and learning at university: enhancing participation and collaboration* (pp. 49-56). Dublin: Research-publishing.net. http://dx.doi.org/10.14705/rpnet.2016.000404

(Hanjani & Li, 2014), and the literature provides evidence for the effectiveness of peer review (e.g. Hu, 2005; Hu & Lam, 2010; Zhao, 2011). However, measuring the impact of such an implementation is not easy (Kleijn et al., 2013). The concept dates back to Vygotsky's (1978) *Zone of Proximal Development* in which students learn from each other by interacting. Such interaction is also observable in the process called *scaffolding* (Weissberg, 2006), where one peer may draw another peer's attention to problematic aspects of a paper that had been overlooked (Ruecker, 2010). The expectation of the FL lecturer is to observe an improvement in the students' writing skills, since this is assumed to be beneficial for both authors and reviewers (Aghaee & Hansson, 2013).

Despite the theoretical benefits of peer review, lecturers need to be cautious of potential drawbacks. Feedback provided by students with limited FL proficiency may be misleading and result in students not trusting 'weak' peers' feedback (Paulus, 1999; Rinehart & Chen, 2012; Rollinson, 2005; Ruecker, 2010; Saito & Fujita, 2004). In this case, a balanced distribution of *asymmetrical feedback*, from a proficient student to a less proficient one, and *symmetrical feedback*, between learners of almost equal skills, should be provided (Hanjani & Li, 2014).

Distribution of student papers is the key element in applying the peer review process. Nowadays, digital technology is a tool at the disposal of writing instructors that not only enables several distribution options but also provides more effective feedback. Going beyond its original aim, *Turnitin*, a plagiarism detector, incorporated the *PeerMark* facility through which students are able to review each other's papers. Since digital peer feedback is a new phenomenon, there is no consensus yet on the superiority of online feedback over traditional modes (Elwood & Bode, 2014).

Digital feedback enables several features not possible in traditional practice. In particular, digital technology can remove student identification for anonymous peer review and provide review tools to students. Thereby, a lecturer can create more effective peer feedback opportunities by eliminating the social constraint of face-to-face feedback (Ho & Savignon, 2007). In the literature, the only study regarding anonymity in a non-digital setting (Robinson, 2002) warns that anonymous peer review may not provide effective feedback if the process is not planned carefully.

2.   The study

As a plagiarism detector, *Turnitin* was successful in reducing the ratio of plagiarism incidents on an academic writing course (Razı, 2014) taught by the researcher of this study. A related study revealed that students were unaware of their real problems since self-reported difficulties did not reflect their actual problems (Razı, 2015). The basic assumption in this study, that of retaining anonymity in the peer review process, is underpinned by Liou and Peng's (2009) study where students were reluctant to highlight their friends' errors. By enabling a balanced distribution of asymmetrical and symmetrical feedback, anonymity may enhance student participation and collaboration in EFL academic writing, leading to the exchange of more effective feedback, and contribute to improved writing skills. The research questions were as follows:

- RQ1: does the digital peer review process work effectively?

- RQ2: should lecturers manage the peer review process openly or anonymously?

- RQ3: should lecturer-feedback precede or follow peer-feedback?

2.1.   Setting and participants

The study was conducted in the English Language Teaching (ELT) department of Canakkale Onsekiz Mart University (COMU), Turkey, in the fall term of 2014. Fifty-nine trainee teacher students who attended the academic writing skills course regularly in three intact classes taught by the researcher were included in the study. They were assigned either to the experimental or control group, based on scores from their first assignment. There were 30 participants (n_{male}=9, n_{female}=21) in the experimental group (anonymous peer review) and 29 participants (n_{male}=9, n_{female}=20) in the control group (open peer review). Independent samples t test did not indicate significant differences between the two groups' mean values on the first assignment. The participants' mean age was 19.

2.2. Materials

As a digital environment, *Turnitin* was used for three basic reasons. Firstly, COMU had an institutional *Turnitin* license, secondly *Turnitin* was superior in detecting plagiarism (Hill & Page, 2009), and thirdly, it enabled peer review facilities.

2.3. Procedures

During the semester, students submitted three different written assignments, each of approximately 500 words. Assignment 1 was used for setting up groups and familiarizing students with the digital peer review process.

In Assignment 2, before matching students, they were grouped into three; namely, 'good', 'moderate', and 'weak', with reference to their scores in Assignment 1. Then, each student received feedback from a 'good', 'moderate', and 'weak' peer; and provided feedback to a 'good', 'moderate', and 'weak' paper.

The students were aware of this categorization but did not know into which category they were placed. They revised their papers and submitted second drafts on which they received lecturer feedback. Then they submitted the final version.

A similar procedure was followed in Assignment 3 with a change. They received lecturer feedback before peer feedback. Following this, they handed in a reflection paper outlining how or if they had benefited from the digital feedback.

3. Findings and discussion

3.1. RQ1: does the digital peer review process work effectively?

The digital peer review facility can be said to work effectively in a digital online environment where lecturers and students are both familiar with the digital tools involved. However, to facilitate the process, *Turnitin* should enable the grouping of students according to writing proficiency and then provide multiple matching from each group since matching students manually is a very complicated task for the lecturer.

3.2. RQ2: should lecturers manage the peer review process openly or anonymously?

Independent samples *t*-test results did not indicate significant differences between the experimental and control group's mean scores on either the second or third assignments. However, data from reflection papers revealed that students preferred digital feedback in comparison to manual. In addition, the participants indicated their preference for feedback from multiple peers, not just a single person. This is invaluable both for the author and reviewer (Aghaee & Hansson, 2013). Good students in particular indicated they did not benefit from single-peer reviews. Regarding open peer review, they emphasised that they avoided criticizing their peers since it felt like giving feedback to a friend. However, when it came to anonymous peer review, they felt like a teacher giving feedback to a student. Thus, students' relations with their classmates have an impact on the quality of feedback in open peer review. Giving feedback also contributes to the classroom management skills of these trainee teachers.

3.3. RQ3: should lecturer-feedback precede or follow peer-feedback?

Data from reflection papers highlighted that students preferred lecturer feedback after peer feedback, not before it. Such a preference emphasises the dominant role of the lecturer, as students prefer final responsibility to be with someone in authority rather than a friend. Students also mentioned that receiving lecturer-feedback helped them appreciate peer-feedback.

4.   Conclusion and implications

Firstly, the digital environment used (*Turnitin*) facilitates the management of exchanging feedback. Considering the first-year undergraduates' inexperience in academic writing, enabling multiple digital feedback would be beneficial.

Secondly, the most important contribution of digital feedback is the possibility of exchanging feedback anonymously. This enables students to make a more honest critique of each others' work. Otherwise, while exchanging peer-feedback openly, they withhold commenting on their peers' weaknesses to avoid problems in daily relations. Moreover, anonymous peer-feedback should be provided from several peers selected in accordance with their writing proficiency. Single-matches can be demotivating due to the risk of being matched with a less proficient peer who cannot provide beneficial feedback.

Finally, lecturer feedback should be provided after peer feedback. Participants' comments indicated this makes them feel much safer. In sum, a combination of "self-, peer, and tutor [review is needed] to help students make informed decisions about [revising] their early drafts and [reflecting] upon the strengths and weaknesses of their writing development" (Lam, 2013, p. 446).

5.   Acknowledgements

My very special thanks go to Graham Lee for language editing the earlier version of the manuscript.

References

Aghaee, N., & Hansson, H. (2013). Peer portal: quality enhancement in thesis writing using self-managed peer review on a mass scale. *The International Review of Research in Open and Distance Learning, 14*(1), 186-203.

Elwood, J. A., & Bode, J. (2014). Student preferences vis-à-vis teacher feedback in university EFL writing classes in Japan. *System, 42,* 333-343. http://dx.doi.org/10.1016/j.system.2013.12.023

Hanjani, A. M., & Li, L. (2014). Exploring L2 writers' collaborative revision interactions and their writing performance. *System, 44,*101-114. http://dx.doi.org/10.1016/j.system.2014.03.004

Hill, J. D., & Page, E. F. (2009). An empirical research study of the efficacy of two plagiarism-detection applications. *Journal of Web Librarianship, 3*(3), 169-181. http://dx.doi.org/10.1080/19322900903051011

Ho, M. C., & Savignon, S. J. (2007). Face-to-face and computer-mediated peer review in EFL writing. *CALICO Journal, 24*(2), 269-290.

Hu, G. (2005). Using peer review with Chinese ESL student writers. *Language Teaching Research, 9*(3), 321-342. http://dx.doi.org/10.1191/1362168805lr169oa

Hu, G., & Lam, S. T. E. (2010). Issues of cultural appropriateness and pedagogical efficacy: exploring peer review in a second language writing class. *Instructional Science, 38*(4), 371–94. http://dx.doi.org/10.1007/s11251-008-9086-1

Kleijn, R. A. M., Mainhard, M. T., Meijer, P. C., Brekelmans, M., & Pilot, A. (2013). Master's thesis projects: student perceptions of supervisor feedback. *Assessment & Evaluation in Higher Education, 38*(8), 1012-1026. http://dx.doi.org/10.1080/02602938.2013.777690

Lam, R. (2013). The relationship between assessment types and text revision. *ELT Journal, 67,* 446-458. http://dx.doi.org/10.1093/elt/cct034

Liou, H. C., & Peng, Z. Y. (2009). Training effects on computer-mediated peer review. *System, 37*(3), 514-525. http://dx.doi.org/10.1016/j.system.2009.01.005

Paulus, T. M. (1999). The effect of peer and teacher feedback on student writing. *Journal of Second Language Writing, 8*(3), 265-289. http://dx.doi.org/10.1016/S1060-3743(99)80117-9

Razı, S. (2014). *Plagiarism detectors in undergraduate academic writing assignments.* Paper presented at the 14th International Language, Literature and Stylistics Symposium, 15-17 October, İzmir, Turkey.

Razı, S. (2015). Cross-checked problems in undergraduate academic writing. In K. Dikilitaş, R. Smith, & W. Trotman (Eds.), *Teacher researchers in action* (pp. 147-161). Kent. IATEFL.

Rinehart, D., & Chen, S. J. (2012). *The benefits of a cycle of corrective feedback on L2 writing: improving Taiwanese technological university students' English writing proficiency.* Saarbrücken, Germany: Lambert Academic Publishing.

Robinson, J. M. (2002). In search of fairness: an application of multi-reviewer anonymous peer review in a large class. *Journal of Further and Higher Education, 26*(2), 183-192. http://dx.doi.org/10.1080/03098770220129451

Rollinson, P. (2005). Using peer feedback in the ESL writing class. *ELT Journal, 59*(1), 23-31. http://dx.doi.org/10.1093/elt/cci003

Ruecker, T. (2010). The potential of dual-language cross-cultural peer review. *ELT Journal, 65*(4), 398-407. http://dx.doi.org/10.1093/elt/ccq067

Saito, H., & Fujita, T. (2004). Characteristics and user acceptance of peer rating in EFL writing classrooms. *Language Teaching Research, 8*(1), 31-54. http://dx.doi.org/10.1191/1362168804lr133oa

Vygotsky, L. S. (1978). *Mind in society: the development of higher psychological processes.* Cambridge, MA: Harvard University Press.

Weissberg, R. (2006). Scaffolded feedback: theoretical conversations with advanced L2 writers. In K. Hyland & F. Hyland (Eds), *Feedback in second language writing: Contexts and issues* (pp. 246-265). Cambridge: Cambridge University Press. http://dx.doi.org/10.1017/CBO9781139524742.015

Zhao, H. (2014). Investigating teacher-supported peer assessment for EFL writing. *ELT Journal, 68*(2), 155-168. http://dx.doi.org/10.1093/elt/cct068

Section 2.

Exploring digital tools and online environments

7 Students as producers and collaborators: exploring the use of padlets and videos in MFL teaching

Anna de Berg[1]

Abstract

In today's digital age, Languages graduates need more specific skills than fluency in the foreign language and intercultural competence. Employers expect from all applicants a high level of computer literacy and a set of soft skills such as creativity or the ability to solve problems and work on team projects. Modern Foreign Language (MFL) departments should therefore promote teaching techniques that would enable their graduates to become employable, at the same time ensuring that the students become aware of their own professional and personal development. This article provides an example of projects concentrated specifically on development of technology and media skills.

Keywords: project-based learning, padlets, foreign languages.

1. Introduction

There is widespread agreement in MFL studies that a conception of teaching and learning as knowledge transfer no longer meets the demands of society in the digital age: today, linguistic competence, even when enhanced by intercultural sensitivity, is not sufficient to prepare Language students for the technological complexity and economic competitiveness of life after graduation. What is needed

1. Sheffield Hallam University, Sheffield, UK; A.deBerg@shu.ac.uk

How to cite this chapter: De Berg, A. (2016). Students as producers and collaborators: exploring the use of padlets and videos in MFL teaching. In C. Goria, O. Speicher, & S. Stollhans (Eds), *Innovative language teaching and learning at university: enhancing participation and collaboration* (pp. 59-64). Dublin: Research-publishing.net. http://dx.doi.org/10.14705/rpnet.2016.000405

are didactic approaches that enable our students to become active participants in a multimedia environment and attractive partners in the global workplace. The question of how to integrate MFL teaching with student production, media orientation and employability has therefore become central to curriculum planning. Against this backdrop, this case study explores the potential of padlets and student-produced videos in a content-based undergraduate (UG) module on German Business, Society and Culture.

2.   Curricular context

The projects (padlets and videos) were conducted in the academic year 2014/15 in a content-based UG module German Business, Society and Culture 1 (BSC 1). In the seminar group, there were 15 students. The module's main purpose is to raise cultural and business awareness of German speaking countries and to prepare the students for their study and work placements abroad. The programme of the module encompasses topics in German history, politics, economy and culture. As is the case with all universities in the UK, Sheffield Hallam's language degree programmes offer the third year abroad as part of the degree provision, but Hallam students spend also a compulsory semester studying at a foreign university in semester 2 of the second year. The period of residence abroad is thus extended to 18 months in total, and the BSC 1 module plays a vital role in familiarising the students with contemporary social and cultural issues in Germany, as well as delivering a practical training in cross-cultural awareness.

3.   Padlets

A padlet (www.padlet.com) is a virtual pin board where students can upload a variety of files, including Word documents, YouTube videos, PowerPoint presentations, etc. It is a collaborative tool, which means that everyone with a link to the pin board can access it and add their comments. I introduced padlets at the beginning of semester 1 as an alternative to the Virtual Learning Environment (VLE) Blackboard. The aims and objectives of the project were:

a) to involve students in a collaborative learning project; b) to engage them in a dialogue outside the classroom; c) to allow them to research the course topics in more detail and share the outcomes with the other students; and d) to create a digital module repository.

I started using padlets for homework, i.e. every week, I created a separate padlet with a few questions about the content of the seminar and asked my students to research the topic in more detail at home and answer the questions in a few lines. The padlets are, by default, anonymous, but I asked my students to sign every homework post. This was also a step that reduced the possibility of a misuse of the platform by posting inappropriate comments.

I encouraged the students to attach links to relevant videos, interesting articles or pictures to make the content more appealing (for more complex analysis of the change processes in communicative practices and the shift from writing to image, see Kress, 2003). The main aim behind this was to create a social platform for a dialogue outside the classroom, where students could interact with each other. The online learning collaboration in this sense can motivate individuals to do more (Davies, 2010) – research a topic in more depth, but also try to improve the language (grammar and vocabulary), as the posts – answers or comments to other answers – are read by other students in the group, not only by the tutor. After a couple of pilot weeks, I started correcting the grammar and style of the posts, and because all students could see every post including my corrections, they started reading my comments more carefully, and learning from each other's mistakes (as they reiterated informally on several occasions).

This process of familiarising with the online tool and the autonomous research activity in a foreign language led to the next step in the padlet project: I asked my students to create their own padlets after my lecture on German film. They were asked to choose a film from the lecture and, based on the information from the lecture and a chapter from *A New History of German Cinema* (Kapczynski & Richardson, 2012), create a padlet about this film. The task they were presented with was to create a visually attractive padlet with only partial information about their chosen film: the students received a handout with several questions about the films. The rationale behind it was to create a module repository with German films, created by the current students for the prospective students. We have now 15 padlets with seminal German films; next year, my new BSC 1 German cohort will receive another set of questions and will continue the work of this year's group. At the moment, it is anticipated that the project will take another two years to complete. The ultimate aim would be to collect the links to the padlets and disseminate them through the German Studies Network after the completion of the project.

4.   Videos

In semester 2, I coordinated two workshops on intercultural awareness, during which my students had to design a cultural briefing session for incoming Erasmus students. In preparation for the workshops, the students were asked to make videos in groups of 5. The aims and objectives of this project were: a) to involve students in a collaborative media project; b) to engage them in a discussion about cultural differences; and c) to prepare them for the experience of studying at a foreign university. The videos were meant to serve as an invitation to a discussion about cultural differences and concentrate on the ideas of "British" vs. "Foreign". In the end, my students produced two 2-minute long videos, which were presented at the opening of the workshops. As part of the project, the students wrote the script for their videos, translated the text into German, filmed themselves in different locations and edited the video, adding stills, captures and other elements.

5.   Evaluation of the survey and conclusion

After both projects and the workshops, I conducted a survey, which was designed to answer, among others, the following questions:

- Do the students now feel more employable?

- Are they more technologically advanced?

I prepared a questionnaire that would highlight potential benefits or shortcomings of the projects. The results showed that the majority of my students had never worked with padlets before or made or edited a video. The overall rating of the course was very high: on the scale 1-5 where 5 indicated the highest level of enjoyment, six students gave it a 4 and seven marked it with 5.

The problem, however, appeared in the questions about employability and technology skills: the majority of the students answered these questions with "I don't know" instead of the expected "definitely agree" or "mostly agree", which brings me to the conclusion and signifies a broader problem: the Languages students are often not aware of the skills and attributes they gain throughout their studies. Jocelyn Wyburd's (2011) report *The Languages Graduate* lists in a form of a grid all linguistic, cultural (and intercultural), employment-specific and personal skills that MFL students develop throughout their course. It is our role as tutors to make sure that our students are aware of these skills and are able to articulate this knowledge in a job interview. It is more than just a thorough knowledge of the foreign country or its language that the Languages graduates can offer to a future employer. As it was in the case of my students, it is a whole set of skills: the ability to collaborate in an online environment, conduct research in a foreign language, plan and conduct a media-project in a team where time is of the essence, and, last but not least, understand the differences and mediate between cultures. I plan to continue with the padlet projects in the next academic year and I will take the video projects further, but plan to engage my students in a discussion about the key employability skills so that they can fully understand, appreciate and articulate the benefits that come with projects like these in order to gain advantage on the highly competitive job market.

References

Davies, J. (2010). A Space for play: crossing boundaries and learning online. In V. Carrington & M. Robinson (Eds.), *Digital literacies: social learning and classroom practices* (pp. 27-41). London: Sage.

Kapczynski, M., & Richardson, M. D. (2012). *A new history of German cinema*. Rochester, New York: Camden House.

Kress, G. (2003). *Literacy in the new media age*. London: Routledge.

Wyburd, J. (2011). *The Languages graduate*. University Council of Modern Languages. Retrieved from http://www.ucml.ac.uk/shapingthefuture/employability

8 Can Facebook or wikis hook learners instead of the schoolbook?

Fakhreddine Brahmi[1]

Abstract

In this paper I will report on a personal experimentation with Facebook and wikis as collaborative learning tools. The aims of implementing these strategies were to develop students' writing skills and to change their attitudes towards learning in the digital age. I delved into this research because I do believe that learning in the new millennium has grown beyond the boundaries of the four walls of the classroom. I have a strong conviction that informal learning through networks is a significant additional (if not an alternative) environment for language practice and use. Having in mind that Facebook is currently considered as a popular means of entertainment among students and wikis are trendy among teachers, I have tried to integrate both in an educational project with pre-determined learning objectives and outcomes.

Keywords: Facebook, wiki, digital writing, collaborative learning, students' attitudes.

1. Introduction

The present study focuses on 2 groups of Tunisian students' perceptions of using Facebook and wikis to develop their writing skills. It is worth noting here that the status quo of teaching at the University of Gafsa as well at other Tunisian

1. University of Gafsa, Tunisia; theenglishclub79@yahoo.fr

How to cite this chapter: Brahmi, F. (2016). Can Facebook or wikis hook learners instead of the schoolbook? In C. Goria, O. Speicher, & S. Stollhans (Eds), *Innovative language teaching and learning at university: enhancing participation and collaboration* (pp. 65-72). Dublin: Research-publishing.net. http://dx.doi.org/10.14705/rpnet.2016.000406

universities urged me to do this empirical study. In fact, Students no longer bring their books/copybooks to the classroom and no longer do the assigned homework. Another issue is the time devoted to the writing sessions, which is not enough to develop their writing skills.

This set off my curiosity to undertake the present study in addition to positive claims towards technology integration like those of Johnson, Levine, Smith, & Smythe (2009) who advocate that "[t]oday, advances in technology have connected students with more information and people than at any other time in human history" (cited in Taranto, Dalbon, & Gaetano, 2011, p. 12), thus "challenging and changing the way we teach" (Bauleke & Herrmann, 2010, p. 33).

2.   Literature review

In addition to the earlier established learning theories, behaviourism, cognitivism, and constructivism, a new theory called connectivism was introduced in 2005. Learning in the digital age has become experiential, rapid, changing and emerges from collaboration and competition, and web 2.0 technologies are viewed as "versatile, affordable, and widely available" (Taranto et al., 2011, p. 13, see also Kisber, Stewart, & Mitchell, 2013).

2.1.   Why Facebook?

In the Tunisian context, Facebook is the forerunner social networking platform. It "contributes to unintentional or unplanned learning that results from other activities, regardless of [whether] those activities are academic or non academic" (Kerka, 2000, cited in Kabilan, Ahmad, & Zainol Abidin, 2010, p. 181).

Additionally, Abbitt (2007) states that there has been "tremendous growth in the popularity of websites focusing on social activities and collaboration" (p. 1); this would include platforms such as Facebook. Selwyn (2009) also "claims that Facebook reflects a good model of learning by its collaborative and active participatory roles of its users" (cited in Mansor et al., 2014, p. 16).

Furthermore, Kabilan et al. (2010) agree with Godwin-Jones's (2008) point of view that tools like Facebook help to a great extent to upgrade correspondence and human connection, can conceivably be tackled for the sake of learning and mastering languages, and have become new sites for potential research (Bloch, 2008).

2.2. Why wikis?

The second type of digital platforms I opted for is wikis. They allow students to "work together to compose a single, collaboratively authored document, or they help each other with their own individual documents" (Morgan & Smith, 2008, p. 80).

According to Ribble (2009),

> "[a] wiki is a collaborative website composed of the continuous cooperative work of many authors. [... A] wiki allows anyone to edit, delete, or modify content that has been placed on the website using a browser interface" (pp. 148-149).

Moreover, Kane and Fichman (2009) "propose that wikis replace textbooks by utilizing available content" (cited in Te'eni, 2009, p. 20), which can make communication easier among educators and students.

3.   Method of the study

Since I intended to explore the perceptions of tertiary-level learners regarding the evolution of their writing and collaborative skills, a quantitative paradigm seemed a suitable approach to the study.

3.1.   Participants

I opted for having 2 groups of 1st year university students of English. Both study writing strategies once a week. The total number of students in these groups is 60. The first, composed of 27, used Facebook, while 33 students in the second group used a wiki. The age range was between 19 and 22. As far as gender is concerned, there were 47 girls and 13 boys.

3.2.   Materials and procedures

Two different questionnaires were administered to the participants in each group before the start of the study. It lasted one semester and by its end, my students were asked to fill in two distinct surveys: one for each group to see whether their attitudes have changed or not after using Facebook and Wikis and if they were helpful in developing their writing skills.

Prior to the administration of the questionnaires, I had meetings with the participants, I explained the purpose and content of the experiment and maintained that their identity and the information they provide would be handled confidentially. Finally, I stated that they could also choose not to partake in this study and leave it at whatever time they so wished (Dowling & Brown, 2010; Heighman & Croker, 2009).

4.   Results and data analysis

Based on the data collected from the questionnaires and surveys, I will present the results first in terms of statistics, and then I will delve into the analysis taking into account the objectives of the study.

4.1.   Facebook vs wiki

73% have been part of the Facebook community for more than 3 years. Just 5% had an account on a wiki before the beginning of this study.

During the study, 68% of the students stated that they log on to Facebook very frequently: At least once a day and for more than 2 hours/day and 27% log on twice or 3 times a week; whereas 32% log on and use wikis in their own time.

While 72% of the total number of students who joined the Facebook group actively participated in the group by posting/commenting, 59% did so in the wiki group.

Out of the total number of the two groups:

- 72% said that the classroom writing session is not enough to develop their writing skills.

- 7% said they write from time to time in English outside the classroom (SMSs or chat).

- 63% admitted having difficulties in writing and these vary from one student to another.

- 84% showed readiness to develop their writing skills through digital tools. In fact, I have noticed that my students' attitudes went through a noticeable change: they became more willing to write and more productive.

- 91% considered the feedback from their peers and the teacher supportive and boosted their confidence, further motivating them to interact and write.

4.2. Facebook and wikis vs classroom

Fascinatingly, while technology is often said to generate seclusion, most of the students seemed to feel that using Facebook or the wiki had the contrary effect when compared with traditional, teacher-led classes, the students again responded quite positively.

- 69% of my students said they prefer digital writing tools. According to them, "learning with technology is always fun".

- 82% of them concurred they like using technology.

A broader analysis revealed that some shy and introvert students partook in the activities in both platforms more than in the classroom.

5.   Discussion

The results of the data analysis reveal that the participants, after a certain time, look at their cohort as a family. Inozu (2010) states that if the group is really coherent, "students become more motivated to interact and this contributes to a creation of a positive group dynamic that increases the effectiveness of lessons" (p. 1061). Ushioda (2003), however, draws attention to the negative effects of "peer group influences and classroom counter-cultures" (p. 97) and points out how these can end up in collective demotivation and collective disaffection.

In fact, what I remarked throughout this study supports Inozu's (2010) view. My students have shown a noticeable inclination to collaborate via digital environments that aim at liberating learners from the somehow repressive immediacy of the classroom.

Finally, as opposed to the claims of "death of the teacher" in the digital age, the participants emphasised the important role of the teacher in guiding them and motivating them and in creating a good group climate.

6.   Conclusion

Based on the data and students' views in this study, Facebook and wikis have been shown to boost confidence, motivate and foster learning and hook students.

Perhaps with such digital tools, our students who are increasingly web 2.0 proficient will become managers of their learning with the help of peers and teachers.

Unfortunately, educators have been slow to recognise the importance of digital literacy and the potential of such platforms as tools for learning has not been fully tapped into by English as a second or foreign language stakeholders.

Amid this fervour to use technologies, teachers must not neglect the pedagogical side. However, we have to upgrade our skills, update our knowledge and change our traditional teaching practices. Within this preview, Prensky (1998) states that "[w]e must get our teachers – hard as it may be in some cases – to stop lecturing, and start allowing students to learn by themselves" (p. 3).

References

Abbitt, J. (2007). Exploring the educational possibilities for a user-driven social content system in an undergraduate course. *MERLOT: Journal of Online Learning and Teaching, 3*(4), 437-447.

Bauleke, D., & Herrmann, K. (2010). Reaching the "iBored". *Middle School Journal, 41*(3), 33-38.

Bloch, J. (2008). From the special issue editor. *Language Learning & Technology, 12*(2), 2-6.

Dowling, P., & Brown, A. (2010). *Doing research/reading research* (2nd ed.). London and New York: Routledge.

Godwin-Jones, R. (2008). Mobile computing technologies: lighter, faster, smarter. *Language Learning & Technology, 12*(3), 3-9

Heighman, J., & Croker, R. A. (2009). *Qualitative research in applied linguistics*. New York: Palgrave Macmillan.

Inozu, J. (2010). The issue of cohesiveness in foreign language classes at higher education. *World Applied Sciences Journal, 10*(9), 1061-1065.

Johnson L., Levine, A., Smith, R., & Smythe, T. (2009). *The 2009 Horizon report: 2009 K-12 edition.* Austin, TX: The New Media Consortium.

Kabilan, M. K., Ahmad, N., & Zainol Abidin, M. J. (2010). Facebook: an online environment for learning of English in institutions of higher education? *The Internet and Higher Education, 13*(4), 179-187. http://dx.doi.org/10.1016/j.iheduc.2010.07.003

Kane, G., & Fichman, R. (2009). The Shoemaker's children: using wikis for information systems teaching, research, and publication. *MIS Quarterly, 33*(1), 1-17.

Kerka, S. (2000). *Incidental learning.* No. 18. Columbus, OH: ERIC Clearinghouse on Adult, Career and Vocational Education.

Kisber, L. B., Stewart, M., & Mitchell, D. (2013). Teaching and learning in the digital world: possibilities and challenges. *LEARNing Landscapes, 6*(2). Retrieved from http://www.learninglandscapes.ca/archives/112-spring-2013-vol6-no2-teaching-and-learning-in-the-digital-world-possibilities-and-challenges

Mansor, N. et al. (2014). Social media in ESL classroom: exploring the impact on language learning. *Journal of Business and Social Development, 2*(1), 14-18. Retrieved from http://rmc.umt.edu.my/wp-content/uploads/sites/53/2014/08/2.-Social-Media.pdf?

Morgan, B., & Smith, R. (2008). A wiki for classroom writing. *The Reading Teacher, 62*(1), 80-82. http://dx.doi.org/10.1598/RT.62.1.10

Prensky, M. (1998). The role of technology in teaching and the classroom. *Educational Technology*, November–December, 1-3.

Ribble, M. (2009). *Raising a digital child: a digital citizenship handbook for parents.* Washington, DC: Home Page Books.

Selwyn, N. (2009). Faceworking: exploring students' education-related use of Facebook. *Learning, Media & Technology, 34*(2), 157-174. http://dx.doi.org/10.1080/17439880902923622

Taranto, G., Dalbon, M., & Gaetano, J. (2011). Academic social networking brings Web 2.0 technologies to the middle grades. *Middle School Journal.* Retrieved from http://cmsd.k12.pa.us/cmsd/cm_intsafe/documents/MiddleSchoolJournalArticleMay2011.pdf?

Te'eni, D. (2009). Comment: the wiki way in a hurry - the ICIS anecdocted. *MIS Quarterly, 33*(1), 20-22.

Ushioda, E. (2003). *Motivation as a socially mediated process.* In D. J. R. Little & E. Ushioda (Eds.), *Learner autonomy in the foreign language classroom: learner, teacher, curriculum and assessment.* Dublin: Authentik.

9 "Become a reporter", the Four Skills News Project: applying and practising language skills using digital tools for level C1/C2 students

Hanna Magedera-Hofhansl[1]

Abstract

The Four Skills News Project is an example of communicative language learning, developed for final year German students at the University of Liverpool. It focuses on how students use and practise their reading, writing, listening and speaking skills via the creative use of news reports and digital technology. Each student creates an avatar using an interactive platform, practicing speaking and correct pronunciation with the help of autocue and thereby enhances his or her language learning experience. Through listening, writing and their own research, students also practise their translating skills. In the final stage of this project, students present their own news item and this also gives them the opportunity to practise their presentation and speaking skills using autocue. Students are filmed and get valuable feedback on their performance in addition to having done something completely new and different that is fun in their final semester at university.

Keywords: digital learning, independent learning, reporter skills, rhetorical skills.

1. University of Liverpool, United Kingdom; hofhansl@liverpool.ac.uk

How to cite this chapter: Magedera-Hofhansl, H. (2016). "Become a reporter", the Four Skills News Project: applying and practising language skills using digital tools for level C1/C2 students. In C. Goria, O. Speicher, & S. Stollhans (Eds), *Innovative language teaching and learning at university: enhancing participation and collaboration* (pp. 73-78). Dublin: Research-publishing.net. http://dx.doi.org/10.14705/rpnet.2016.000407

1.   Introduction

In language teaching, our aim is that students master receptive, productive as well as mediative skills. But how can we achieve this as language tutors? The following article describes a creative and interactive project for students in level C1 and C2 according to the Common European Framework of Reference for Languages, where students can practise all of the above language skills[2].

Fast-moving technologies define our age, but we as staff or so-called digital immigrants are probably going to be at least one step behind our students or so-called digital natives (Prensky, 2001) when it comes to knowledge about the latest Information Technology (IT). We can, however, try to implement some digital tools in our language teaching and students' language learning[3].

Applying these two elements, new technologies and various language skills, is the main purpose of the Four Skills News Project. This is done in German at the University of Liverpool, but it can be adapted to any foreign language. It can be either an assessed or a formative exercise. The Four Skills News Project is designed to be taught in weeks 3, 6 and 10 of the second semester to build up practical language competence, although each of the three components can be used individually.

The receptive skills of reading and listening are practised by researching articles and close-listening and transcribing a short news clip. The productive skills, writing and speaking, are applied when students prepare their own news clip, and the mediative skills, translating and consecutive interpreting as well as summarising texts from one language into another are used when learners research the website of their home university and prepare it in the target language and thereby create a news item.

---

2. http://www.coe.int/t/dg4/linguistic/cadre1_en.asp

3. The Four Skills News Project was developed by Hanna Magedera-Hofhansl at the University of Liverpool from 2011 and enhanced by digital resources mentioned in 'Listen, Speak, Read, Write Web', a workshop given by Joe Dale at the University of Liverpool on 9th February 2015.

In the Four Skills News Project language learners practise and apply all four language skills: reading, writing, listening and speaking acquired over the first few years at university. The student-produced news clips are recorded on film and can be put on a website.

2.   Create a journalist avatar

This project is based around current affairs. In the languages lab, students first listen to a one-minute audio news clip in the target language chosen by their language tutors. In German, we use Deutsche Welle as this website offers a slowly spoken version of news. This allows listeners to take notes and the lab facilities allow them to listen to the audio as many times as necessary. This is a good warm-up exercise to get students used to a lab setting and to listening attentively. At the same time, they can research a similar topic using online newspapers to find technical terms, regionalisms or any other vocabulary relevant to this topic. Students are then asked to write a summary of the news in the target language and check their spelling and grammar. Distributing in advance a list of frequent mistakes such as verb-noun agreement and syntax helps students be more precise in their writing skills.

When finished, the summary can be animated by an avatar using the website www.voki.com. This tool is very user-friendly, students simply click on 'create', select the language and give their avatars a face, then use the key with the 'T' (for text) on it to give it a voice. After pasting in the summary into the textbox and making sure that all components are satisfactory, it can be published. This creates a weblink that can be put on the interactive padlet platform. By double-clicking on the wall and entering the first name only (as it is publicly accessible) everybody's voki weblink can be added on the padlet. Students can be encouraged to listen to classmates' news summaries. The avatars are fun and simple to create and they take away the embarrassment of hearing one's own voice while still being able to listen to correct pronunciation despite the robot-like demeanour.

3.   The news presenter's body language

As a next step in preparation for class in week 6, learners are required to imitate a native speaker news reporter. In their own time, students choose any one-minute news item in their target language that interests them. This is a good opportunity for students doing joint honours degrees to practise vocabulary relevant to their second subject, e.g. business, law, history, etc. Students take notes and transcribe the text; this requires accurate listening skills. When they have finished, they should practise reading the news using the correct intonation, imitate the reporter's rhythm, tone of voice and facial expressions. The objective is to imitate the actual reporter as closely as possible. Another part of this exercise is to use the reporter's gestures and demeanour. Students can choose news clips from different areas or countries. With the German language, it could also be with a Swiss or Austrian accent, which makes particular sense if students have spent their year abroad there. This is entirely acceptable, as long as it is consistent.

Learners record themselves either in the languages lab or at home with their electronic devices until they are happy with the result. If there are uncertainties with regards to content and comprehension, it helps if they read newspaper articles in the target language relevant to this topic. This will give them additional information and relevant vocabulary or technical terms. These articles need to go into the bibliography. Students should email their text and the links used to themselves so that they can copy and paste them into an autocue website in the languages lab. With new words, we recommend that students listen to them several times on online dictionaries to be confident when saying them.

In class in week 6, students present their news using an autocue tool on the cueprompter website which lets them choose the speed at which they read and makes for a more natural recording. When students listen to their recording, they should also analyse what they would do differently. Once they are happy, the recording could be put on a voki avatar and added to the padlet. Again, it is also fun for them to listen to their classmates' news reports.

4. Putting it all into practice: the student news report

Language learners are asked to prepare and write their own news report. The crucial part is research. So as to avoid the temptation to cut and paste, we recommend that students research what is going on at their own university from the homepage or from the university blogs. Chances are that the university's internal news will not exist on a news platform in the target language, so students will have to create their own piece of news after having researched in English. Students summarise English news in the target language. Students also need to be aware that news items are formal, but in a spoken register, therefore sentences need to be short enough to be understood by any listener. Again, students can choose a topic that interests them and that is related to their degree. Links must be put in a bibliography. Students prepare a one-minute news report in the target language now applying the vocabulary and phrases that they have acquired during their research. Important parts are also a greeting, transition and an end to the news item which they can copy from actual news broadcasts they have previously listened to. After practising speaking it and learning it by heart, it can be presented in class, or students can use the autocue again. The essential part here is to use the correct demeanour and gestures, tone of voice and the language cadences, the correct pronunciation, register and grammar. After first using an avatar with and without their voice, students at Liverpool are now filmed in class. They can now show that they are confident speaking and being a reporter. They can use the autocue programme if learning their text by heart is too difficult. Dressing formally helps for this exercise and boosts their confidence. This can be assessed as an oral exam. Alternatively, the whole project can be assessed as a portfolio.

The emphasis on pronunciation and speech in this project is not a general remedy for all ills, and it will not make students speak with a perfect accent forever, but they learn to self-diagnose mistakes and to correct errors.

If put on a website, it also gives an interesting news stream in the target language about what is happening at their alma mater. It shows a good range of student representation that is inspiring for prospective students and it is useful for open days and the like. Professional presentation skills are important for employability This project can either be formative or summative. As an assessment, individual components can be evaluated, or the progress can be put in a portfolio, or the last component can be assessed as an oral exam.

In conclusion, the above application of the Four Skills News Project is like a cooking recipe that can be used to inspire any tutor to use its method (or ingredients) to make his or her own creations. This application of the project foregrounds creativity within a strict set of parameters that enhances students' confidence in the foreign language. Encouraging final-year students to work collaboratively in this way is a welcome respite from their focus on their degree results. This may have a positive outcome on the way that the students view their final year of university.

5.   Acknowledgements

I would like to thank Laura Root for proof-reading my manuscript.

Reference

Prensky, M. (2001). Digital natives, digital immigrants. *On the Horizon, 9*(5), 1-6. http://dx.doi.org/10.1108/10748120110424816

Useful websites

Deutsche Welle (German news, spoken slowly): http://www.dw.de
http://voki.com to create avatars
https://padlet.com to create an interactive platform
http://cueprompter.com to use the autocue feature

10 Transmedia teaching framework: from group projects to curriculum development

James Reid[1] and Filippo Gilardi[2]

Abstract

This paper describes an innovative project-based learning framework theoretically based on the ideas of Transmedia Storytelling, Participatory Cultures and Multiple intelligences that can be integrated into the flipped classroom method, and practically addressed using Content-Based Instruction (CBI) and Project-Based Learning (PBL) approaches. It shows how this framework has been developed and integrated into the Academic Reading curriculum at Akita International University (AIU) in Japan by giving examples of the high quality work students can produce and outlining specific techniques and assessment criteria.

Keywords: transmedia, content-based instruction, project-based learning, flipped classroom, EAP.

1.   Introduction

This paper outlines how the Transmedia teaching method has been implemented in the Academic Reading curriculum at AIU in Japan. Here, the Transmedia method combines the original theoretical framework – Transmedia Storytelling, Participatory Culture and Multiple Intelligences (Reid, Hirata, & Gilardi, 2011) – with elements of flipped classroom, PBL and CBI.

1. Akita International University, Akita, Japan; rjames@aiu.ac.jp

2. University of Nottingham Ningbo China, China; filippo.gilardi@nottingham.edu.cn

How to cite this chapter: Reid, J., & Gilardi, F. (2016). Transmedia teaching framework: from group projects to curriculum development. In C. Goria, O. Speicher, & S. Stollhans (Eds), *Innovative language teaching and learning at university: enhancing participation and collaboration* (pp. 79-84). Dublin: Research-publishing.net. http://dx.doi.org/10.14705/rpnet.2016.000408

2.   Teaching context

AIU's Academic Reading Course requires a TOEFL-ITP score of 500 or higher, and a 12 hour per week, 15 week commitment. The course develops the reading skills and vocabulary needed to complete university-level assignments. It focuses on reading strategies, critical engagement with academic texts, and acquisition of the Academic Word List (Coxhead, 2000).

Formerly, students completed exercises on academic texts to learn lexis and content. However, it was felt that a Confucian-heritage culture of passivity prevailed with too many students adopting a rote-memorization approach to lexis, and a strategic-surface approach to content. In 2013, the Transmedia Teaching method was introduced to challenge this paradigm, with at least five group projects being assigned for each student to work on. From 2014, the method was situated in a flipped learning context, which involved hosting previous semester projects on the Virtual Learning Environment (VLE) for current semester students to learn from. The result was students became more inspired, learned content and lexis more deeply, and became familiar with assessment criteria before producing their own projects.

3.   Transmedia teaching in the context of CBI, PBL and flipped classrooms

Inspired by Transmedia Storytelling (the creation of coherent fictional universes in the entertainment industry), the Transmedia teaching method was developed to promote active participation by empowering students to create learning projects. Just as the various media products of a Hollywood franchise, such as *The Marvel Cinematic Universe*, are accessed to learn more about the fictional world, student-created media projects allow participants and observers to engage in multiple modalities that analyse, synthesize and critically evaluate texts.

The method evolved from a consideration of Gardner's (2011) theory of Multiple Intelligences, that posits people have different learning strengths that can be incorporated into study, and Internet-based participatory cultures in which people, particularly Millennials, feel empowered to create and comment on content. We realized that students who were passive in the classroom were often active in cyberspace, and thus sought to bring this engagement into the classroom (Gilardi & Reid, 2011).

At AIU, the focus is on target language and content, therefore the projects that students created fit the definitions of both CBI and PBL. CBI encourages active, experiential learning that incorporates peer to peer interaction and student-led research. PBL is a "natural extension of CBI" (Stoller, 2002, p. 109) in that it focuses on the learning of contextualised content rather than isolated lexical or grammatical items, is cooperative rather than competitive, integrates skills and information processing, and results in the creation of projects that can stimulate learning (Stoller, 2002).

Since the projects are digitized it seemed useful to host them on the VLE for future cohorts to access, which led to the flipped learning (Bergmann & Sams, 2012) component of the curriculum. Prior to beginning their own projects, students were directed to use the assessment criteria (see Table 1 and Table 2 to critically evaluate the projects created by previous cohorts. This inspired them when creating their own projects as well as helping them learn more deeply.

After three weeks of viewing and evaluating previous projects, each current student was assigned to 5 different randomized groups to create content and vocabulary projects for 5 different academic texts. This resulted in 4 projects a week over the remainder of the semester.

Both Content and Vocabulary groups were required to meet specific requirements (see Table 1 and Table 2). Content projects ranged from PowerPoint or Prezi presentations with embedded media clips, to poster presentations and self-contained videos (e.g. https://goo.gl/okUyWn and https://goo.gl/b5IIxJ). Vocabulary groups often integrated digital presentations with videos and handouts (e.g. https://goo.gl/bN7WlN and https://goo.gl/Khkvyl).

4. Marking criteria and social loafing

Table 1 and Table 2 show the marking criteria used to evaluate the Transmedia projects. Over the three week initial evaluation period, current students used these marking criteria to critically evaluate projects from previous semesters. The instructor would share his/her evaluation of each project to help students understand the criteria in more depth.

Table 1. Content presentation marking criteria

CONTENT Presentation	F		D		C		B		A		
	0-5		12	13	14	15	16	17	18	19	20
REQUIREMENTS •8 highlighted target words used correctly •Chapter Summary •Critical Conclusion •4 Comprehension Questions •3 Critical thinking Questions	Most requirements missing or inadequate.		Some requirements missing or inadequate; unsatisfactory level of understanding and critical thought displayed.		Satisfactory attention to most requirements; average amount of critical thought and understanding demonstrated.		Good attention to all requirements; content solidified and expanded well; good amount of critical thought and understanding demonstrated.		All requirements exceeded; current state of issue, application to outside contexts; and exceptional understanding and critical thought displayed.		
	0-5		6	6.5	7	7.5	8	8.5	9	10	
CREATIVITY & ENGAGEMENT	Little creative effort made; unengaging result.		Only mildly interesting; minimal originality displayed. Many students not able to participate.		Average amount of creativity and engagement. Most students given chance to participate.		Creative content presented in an interesting and engaging manner. Everyone given the chance to participate.		Extraordinary amount of creativity applied; presentation continually active and captivating.		
	0-5		6	6.5	7	7.5	8	8.5	9	10	
ENGLISH	Serious errors render the presentation incomprehensible.		Substantial number of errors impede meaning.		Some errors impede meaning, but presentation is delivered satisfactorily.		A few errors that do not impede meaning; presentation delivered well.		Very few minor errors that do not impede meaning; very professional delivery.		

Since each group member received the same grade they were told to contact their instructor if a group member was under-performing. Although this did not entirely eliminate "Social Loafing" (Lee & Lim, 2012, p. 214), it did reduce its incidence. Additionally, since the instructor consulted with the students as they created their projects, it was possible to monitor the extent to which each group member contributed. Other ways to ensure fairness might include self-evaluation forms, the inclusion of an individual grade, or the capacity for groups to assign percentages to individual members.

Table 2.   Vocabulary activity marking criteria

VOCABULARY Presentation	F		D		C		B		A		
	0-5		12	13	14	15	16	17	18	19	20
REQUIREMENTS •18 target words used correctly in original sentences •Clear instructions given for activities •Solidification of target word knowledge	Most requirements missing or inadequate.		Some requirements missing or inadequate.		Satisfactory attention to most requirements.		Good attention to all requirements; well-constructed activity that solidifies target word knowledge.		All requirements exceeded; Very well-constructed activity that solidifies target word knowledge.		
	0-5		6	6.5	7	7.5	8	8.5	9		10
CREATIVITY & ENGAGEMENT	Presenters did not help students with activity; badly-designed activity lacking creativity.		Activity only mildly interesting; minimal originality displayed. Many students not able to participate.		Activity is quite creative and interesting; most students given chance to participate.		Good level of creativity and engagement achieved. Everyone able to participate.		Extraordinary amount of creativity; original or improved activity resulted in high levels of engagement.		
	0-5		6	6.5	7	7.5	8	8.5	9		10
ENGLISH	English is incomprehensible. Presentation style almost non-existent.		Many errors impede meaning. Unsatisfactory presentation style.		Some errors impede meaning. Satisfactory presentation style.		Errors do not impede meaning; activity delivered well. Good presentation style.		Only a few minor errors; Professional presentation style.		

5.   Conclusion

Flipped classrooms put the onus on individual teachers to choose or create downloadable content. In contrast, the Transmedia model exploits a 'wisdom of the crowds' approach by confidently assuming that Millennials have the requisite skills and technology to create high quality projects. Our experience is that students learn what is possible from evaluating previous students' work and then seek to match or exceed it. We have not observed the prioritisation of group harmony over "cognitive contributions" (Lee & Lim, 2012, p. 219). This could be due to high levels of motivation and/or because the teacher plays an important consulting role. Most students report that their primary motivation becomes intrinsic rather than grade-driven and they consistently produce high quality work. While it is impossible to definitively measure whether students acquire knowledge at a greater rate and depth than students in more traditional settings, it is the case that exam scores have been higher than in previous years, indicating this to be the case. It is also indisputable that this method empowers the student and relieves the burden on the teacher to be the primary vehicle of input. It fosters group cohesion and develops skills that encompass negotiation, technology, authentic L2 use, time-management, research, public speaking, critical thinking and creativity.

References

Bergmann, J., & Sams, A. (2012). *Flip your classroom: reach every student in every class every day*. International Society for Technology in Education.

Coxhead, A. (2000). A new academic word list. *TESOL Quarterly, 34*(2), 213-238.

Gardner, H. (2011). *Frames of mind: the theory of multiple intelligences*. New York: Basic Books.

Gilardi, F., & Reid, J. (2011). E-learning through transmedia storytelling. How the emerging internet-based participatory cultures in China can be co-opted for education. In S. Barton, J. Hedberg & K. Suzuki (Eds.), *Proceedings of global learn 2011* (pp. 1469-1474). Association for the Advancement of Computing in Education (AACE).

Lee, H. J., & Lim, C. (2012). Peer evaluation in blended team project-based learning: what do students find important? *Journal of Educational Technology & Society, 15*(4), 214-224

Reid, J., Hirata, Y., & Gilardi, F. (2011). Student-centred transmedia inspired language learning projects. *ACTC 2011: the Asian conference on technology in the classroom* (pp. 80-96).

Richards, J. C., & Renandya, W. A. (Eds.). (2002). *Methodology in language teaching: an anthology of current practice*. Cambridge: Cambridge University Press.

Stoller, F. (2002). Project work: a means to promote language and content. In J. C. Richards & W. A. Renandya (Eds.), *Methodology in language teaching: an anthology of current practice* (pp. 107-119). Cambridge: Cambridge University Press.

11 Overcoming navigational design in a VLE: students as agents of change

Marion Sadoux[1], Dorota Rzycka[2], Mizuho Jones[3], and Joaquin Lopez[4]

Abstract

This paper focuses on the outcomes of a project funded by the Teaching and Learning Enhancement Office at the University of Nottingham Ningbo China (UNNC). Students were recruited to design a new navigational architecture for the Moodle pages of the Language Centre. They received some training on the key principles of distributive learning and worked with a small team of Language Centre Blended Learning coordinators in a series of rapid prototyping design workshops. The core focus of the project was on creating a suitable navigational architecture which would enable our predominantly Chinese students to engage confidently with our Virtual Learning Environment (VLE) pages and to limit cultural cognitive dissonance as much as possible. The student designs were then vetted by the entire team of tutors and used as the basis for the development of a coherent blended learning plan.

Keywords: virtual learning environment, navigational design, students as agents of change, cultural cognition.

1. University of Nottingham Ningbo China, China; Marion.Sadoux@nottingham.edu.cn

2. University of Nottingham Ningbo China, China; Dorota.Rzycka@nottingham.edu.cn

3. University of Nottingham Ningbo China, China; Mizuho.Jones@nottingham.edu.cn

4. University of Nottingham Ningbo China, China; Joaquin.Lopez@nottingham.edu.cn

How to cite this chapter: Sadoux, M., Rzycka, D., Jones, M., & Lopez, J. (2016). Overcoming navigational design in a VLE: students as agents of change. In C. Goria, O. Speicher, & S. Stollhans (Eds), *Innovative language teaching and learning at university: enhancing participation and collaboration* (pp. 85-91). Dublin: Research-publishing.net. http://dx.doi.org/10.14705/rpnet.2016.000409

1. Project rationale

As many other departments in universities, the Language Centre at UNNC makes use of the University's dedicated VLE platform, Moodle, to support the delivery of all its accredited modules. Not untypically, the implementation of Moodle in the department took place in response to University directives without any concerted reflexion or plan at the local level as to how this VLE might be best used and structured.

The result a few years down the line, is one where adoption is patchy in terms of content design beyond the minimum institutional requirements and where practice varies enormously from sophisticated uses with a co-constructivist distributive delivery framework to the accumulation of learning and teaching materials where the VLE serves as a mere repository. The lack of a concerted adoption or implementation plan has lead to a number of problems greatly reducing the potential benefits in terms of teaching and learning that both language tutors and students could gain from the use of a VLE:

- It is difficult for tutors in large co-taught modules sharing the same Moodle page to appropriate a coherent space or to develop their own instructional practice. These pages tend to either be controlled by the Module Convener or individual tutors develop their content separately on one block – leading to overload, repetition of content and endless downwards vertical development (compare Figure 1 and Figure 2).

- Tutors report a lack of engagement with interactive tools on Moodle and have clear difficulties in getting students to develop an online cognitive presence on the VLE, thereby greatly limiting its potential to facilitate co-constructive learning through fora, blogs or wikis and to play a sufficient role in a distributive learning framework.

- The disparity of practice exists within individual language levels too, meaning that students progressing from one level to the next (90% of our learners) do not follow a logical or habitual structure.

- The feedback from students often contradicts the work carried out by tutors – for instance on numerous Moodle pages where an enormous amount of contents and resources are available, students report a lack of resources.

Figure 1.   Moodle navigation before the project

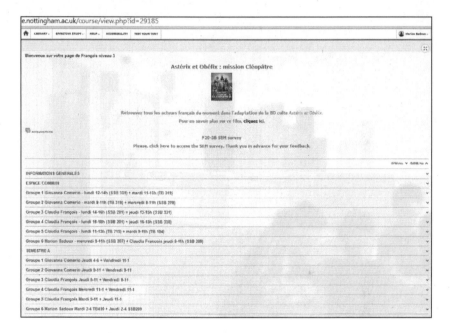

Another important concern underpinning this project focuses on the possible clash between the cultural cognitive styles of our learners (predominantly Chinese) and the Moodle interface which is essentially a 'western' educational product.

In other words, our project sought to work in partnership with our students in order to design a new navigational architecture that would be clear and appealing to them and that could serve as a blueprint for a coherent and cohesive plan to develop the Language Centre's pedagogy in using the VLE.

Figure 2.   The same module with new navigation

2.   Why focus primarily on navigational design?

Studies on web usability all point to navigational design as being of primary importance for users and yet, this is something which is rarely the focus of any training on how to use a VLE or even rarely the focus of any eLearning training, as can be evidenced by glancing at University eLearning training resources. Yet it is of vital importance to pay attention to navigation and to ensure that it is user-friendly. As Thorne pointed out in an interview with Jeanette Campos in 2012,

> "when we talk about [...] instructional design, there is a piece that is routinely overlooked and that most people do poorly. You have to design

navigation. You have to design the navigation before you start developing. It has to be planned. The navigation matters, and it is an element of design that is unique to eLearning. First, plan the navigation. All of the other layers will follow" (para. 11).

Planning the navigation though, requires a clear notion of the elements that learners will need to navigate to and from as well as decisions about the linearity or otherwise multiplicity of pathways that need to be available to learners. In the context of higher education, and particularly within cross faculty non-specialist language learning provision; self-directed learning, lifelong learning and flexibility are key notions in the value of the provision deployed, and as Martínez-Torres, Toral, and Barrero (2011) propose: "[a]t University, the use of [information and communications technology] should be focused on flexibility and self-management" (p. 280).

Both dimensions require the existence of flexible pathways which render the navigational design all the more complex. This flexibility is also related to learner difference and to learner motivation which are both crucial dimensions to consider when designing for language learning. As Hodges (2004) points out, such design requires one to

"make an effort to [make] learners attribute their learning outcomes to the controllable and unstable construct of effort. Learners will have no motivation to participate in a learning experience, without the belief that change is possible. [...] The [design] should allow for choice and self-direction" (pp. 2-4).

Our project focused on navigational design as the central pillar that could enable a positive engagement with Moodle along multiple pathways that individual learners could choose in order to remain sufficiently motivated to invest in successful self–directed learning to supplement face to face teaching. Without a clear navigational design, all such endeavours would lead to disproportionate and possibly unsuccessful orientation efforts that would inevitably undermine our learners' ability to engage.

3. Why students as designers?

There were three main reasons why the project team thought it essential to invite students to design the navigational framework of our Moodle pages, quite aside from the fact that few good products are designed without involving the end users in the process. '

In the first instance, working with students allowed us to challenge our own assumptions and beliefs and it is in that sense that we sought to explore what they could bring to the project as change agents. Secondly, we were concerned that our own perceptions of a Moodle page's architecture might be partial and related to our own ability to read the web. Indeed, many of the Chinese websites our students prefer to refer to for language learning, appear impenetrable to even those of us who can read Chinese, as can be seen in the comparison between the two websites for learning French http://www.lepointdufle.net and http://fr.hujiang.com/. We were therefore keen to question the adaptability of the linear vertical navigation pathway offered almost as a default by standard VLE designs such as Moodle. We were keen to explore the principle according to which web-design has a strong cultural cognitive dimension. As Faiola and Matei (2006) point out,

> "researchers should move away from homogeneous design models and [... should] devise test models that can account for cultural cognition and the influence of cultural context on the cognitive style of web site designers" (p. 389).

4. The project and its outcomes

We worked with a team of eleven students around semi-structured workshops with a strong focus on visual design. Ideas were represented visually rather than verbally. We created 13 Moodle pages, three per language (three levels taught) and one for the project designed by the tutors' team and used for content delivery of training and for communication. Designs were submitted by the lead designers as screencasts where they recorded a narration over their design and uploaded the files as Moodle assignments.

The student designs were closely connected to one another – although one used a 'collapsed topics' structure already in use for the module studied. They chose a horizontal rather than a vertical design structure, which enables a full view of all items in the first page, and opted for a hybrid model of content including both linear pathways and non-linear exploration (self-directed) and enabling clear navigation through the use of drop-down menus.

Subsequently the designs were presented back to the language centre team in a review meeting. One template was chosen (see Figure 2), simplified, deployed to all modules and used to develop our blended learning plan. This was met with strong enthusiasm from some tutors who were genuinely inspired by the student's work and by some reticence from a small number of tutors who were opposed to changing current practice. The majority of language tutors were keen to see Moodle reinvented through the eyes of students and to listen to their ideas as a means to boost learner engagement.

References

Campos, J. (2012). Peeling back the layers: an interview with Kevin Thorn. *eLearn magazine*. Retrieved from http://elearnmag.acm.org/featured.cfm?aid=2170471

Faiola, A., & Matei, S. A. (2006). Cultural cognitive style and web design: beyond a behavioral inquiry into computer-mediated communication. *Journal of computer-mediated communication, 11*(1), 375-394. http://dx.doi.org/10.1111/j.1083-6101.2006.tb00318.x

Hodges, C. B. (2004). Designing to motivate: motivational techniques to incorporate in e-Learning experiences. *Journal of interactive online learning, 2*(3), 1-7. Retrieved from http://www.ncolr.org/jiol/issues/pdf/2.3.1.pdf

Martínez-Torres, M. R., Toral, S. L., & Barrero, F. (2011). Identification of the design variables of eLearning tools. *Interacting with computers, 23*(3), 279-288. http://dx.doi.org/10.1016/j.intcom.2011.04.004

Section 3.

Beyond the language classroom

12 From widening horizons to widening participation: transmitting the experience of global citizenship to the school classroom

Cathy Hampton[1] and Ariane Demeure-Ahearne[2]

Abstract

This paper gives account of a project involving Year Abroad students of French at Warwick University challenged to select *realia* from their host countries in order to stimulate enthusiasm for language learning in local schools. It considers the cognitive and affective processes informing the 'culture gathering' that took place: how did the responsibility to act as the interface between a foreign culture and their own inform these students' own intercultural and linguistic journeys? Assessing outcomes, the paper goes on to describe the implementation of a more ambitious second stage project involving the Routes into Languages Adopt a Class scheme, Warwick PGCE MFL students and staff, and students on the British Council assistantship and Erasmus programmes.

Keywords: year abroad, global citizenship, intercultural, linguistic, university.

1. Introduction

There is something of a paradox in the current situation in Modern Foreign Language (MFL) education in the UK: whilst students in higher education institutions are being encouraged to participate in study abroad initiatives

1. University of Warwick, United Kingdom; C.M.Hampton@warwick.ac.uk

2. University of Warwick, United Kingdom; A.H.Y.Demeure-Ahearne@warwick.ac.uk

How to cite this chapter: Hampton, C., & Demeure-Ahearne, A. (2016). From widening horizons to widening participation: transmitting the experience of global citizenship to the school classroom. In C. Goria, O. Speicher, & S. Stollhans (Eds), *Innovative language teaching and learning at university: enhancing participation and collaboration* (pp. 95-104). Dublin: Research-publishing.net. http://dx.doi.org/10.14705/rpnet.2016.000410

and exchange programmes in order to increase their exposure to a 'global' environment, and to develop 'intercultural' skills highly prized by employers, pupils in UK schools are voting with their feet away from the study of language.

Currently, initiatives to alter the direction of travel, such as compulsory language teaching in primary schools, and the introduction of the English baccalaureate in the secondary sector, have had mixed results. 29% of state secondary schools have seen a reduction in the numbers of hours available for language teaching in the curriculum, and the transition between primary and secondary language learning is far from smooth, limiting the impact of the KS2 initiative (Board & Tinsley, 2015). This disengagement with language surely reduces the impact of other cross-cultural education within the UK classroom. If transcultural competence is intended to enable learners to "reflect on the world and themselves through the lens of another language and culture" (MLA Ad Hoc Committee on Foreign Languages, 2007, para 9), experiencing linguistic difference is paramount, and forces greater engagement with global epistemologies that are challenging traditional national and cultural boundaries. At this febrile moment in the history of education, described by Barnett (2007) as an 'age of uncertainty', new pedagogies are required to form "future citizens of a multicultural society and open economy in a globalised world" (Priestland et al., 2013, para 6).

2.   Engaging the Year Abroad language student as transcultural specialist

This paper describes a practical response to some of these questions that uses the uncertainty of the open space and travel afforded by the Year Abroad as a springboard to cognitive engagement with the language-culture binary in both the school and the university classroom. In a pilot project running from 2013-15, 15 volunteer students about to undertake their intercalated study Year Abroad (13 to France; 2 to Canada) embraced the challenge to seek out *realia* and other artifacts that could be used to bring the contemporary experience of living and working in a French or francophone country directly into the language classroom. The students visited three local schools before departure to gain a sense of current trends in MFL school teaching, and received training on the national curriculum from a MFL PGCE academic. During the Year Abroad, the group used a variety of social media to share and debate their discoveries. On their return, they formed teams around key topics (travel and transport, protest in France, the *bande dessinée*, food and regionalism, local history and tourism, and Québec) and began creating learning activities with their resources, advised by two MFL secondary teachers.

3.   An overview of pedagogical aims and outcomes

In line with Helle, Tynjälä, and Olkinuora's (2006) values of project-based learning, the task of identifying cultural and linguistic artifacts was intended pedagogically to be the "problem [...] serv[ing] to drive learning activities" with "learner control of the learning process" at its centre (pp. 290-292). In this way, the project aimed to make connections between the process of resource gathering, the building of core skills (collaboration, communication, time management), and deep reflection on the labile relationship between language, culture and self. This triangulation worked effectively whilst the students were in their host countries, as they reflected in interviews on their return. Jack, the project leader, summed up:

> "the challenges working with a project that has people so distributed in so many different places, from Canada to different regions in France. Trying to liaise with all those people at the same time and bring deadlines together was quite a useful experience and set of skills to bring into a kind of professional life".

An enriched perception of global identity clearly emerged as the students weighed up the learning potential of the different cultural objects they had chosen. Taking as an example the group's engagement with the *bande dessinée*, online discussions reveal that initially the object itself required some cultural decoding by the students:

> "One idea I was thinking about for this project was the French hardback comic books which seem to be quite popular in France. BD or bande dessinée are the latest craze in my town amongst younger teenagers".

There followed processes of:

- personal identification with the object:

  > "turns out loads of people our age read them too";

- cross-cultural discussion:

  > "when I asked [the children of the family I live with] about this project and their ideas, BD was the resource they thought would work best with people their age in England";

- and engagement with regional practices:

  > "the 41st International Festival of Bande Dessinée is taking place in Angoulême next weekend";

  > "I'll try to find some Quebecois equivalents too[3]".

4. Project ontologies: an overview of key values and aspirations

The students' remit within the scope of the project was to assess the object's characteristics and its possible applications for younger learners, and this

---

3. Quotations taken from forum discussions.

responsibility added complexity to their consideration of its plural functions. Below, Jack discusses this kind of cognitive awakening:

"[You] understand that in some regions there are different languages, different words, different cultural practices: things I hadn't really thought about. You can have so many differences within one country and within one […] culture, it kind of made you aware of just how many cultural differences there could be within a continent. […] It makes you appreciate the sheer scale of it".

Representing the authentic origins of an object became an important component of the project, as Ben noted:

"A lot of the stuff I picked up I would have picked up anyway: it was kind of maps and guides and tickets that I picked up by virtue of living in Paris […] so it was kind of the practical day to day life: it wasn't really a conscious effort all the time, and in some ways I feel that made it a little bit more authentic, because it's a genuine lived experience".

Molly-May, a language assistant, arrived at her lycée to discover pupils on strike as a result of the 'affaire Léonarda' (the controversial expulsion of a Roma girl, removed very publicly from her school by French immigration authorities in October 2013). She simply asked her students to note down their response to the incident (did they all strike? why (not)?), and returned to the UK with an object in the form of a series of testimonies.

Julia joined a French student activist group that offered support, both educational and pastoral, to prisoners. Her learning object was taken from *L'Envolée*, the group's magazine, and was personalised through her experience of visiting in a Parisian prison.

Fi and Gwen, both in Canada, sought to convey the physical effects of their new landscape and its exotic properties: the cold; the different flora and fauna (see Figure 1).

The personal investment in students' chosen learning objects was in no doubt. Furthermore, it was clear that they had begun to "rethink [...] the relationship of 'language' with 'culture' in quite a marked way" (Freadman, 2014, p. 373). Some key values emerged:

- In a digital world, the value to pupils of physical contact with *realia* was paramount: students created hardcopy school resource packs to address this need[4].

- The story behind the *realia* chosen was itself important and could act as a 'hook' to engage pupils: students included a personal fact file in each pack telling their story (see Figure 2 for an example).

- Serendipity was crucial: stimulating materials were discovered in unexpected places. Any future project should continue to embrace the student as producer ethos.

Figure 1.   Fi's and Gwen's learning object

---

4. The resource packs contained accessible realia such as tickets, brochures and maps, together with accompanying worksheets devised by the students (involving, at KS3: role play, matching words to pictures, plotting journeys on maps; and KS4: decoding cursive handwriting; identifying and correcting errors in native speaker French; researching and creating protest slogans; analysing the ethics of the prison system).

Figure 2. Fact file by Ben, one of the Warwick students

(Year abroad spent interning at HEC Paris.)

My name is Ben and I am a final year student studying French & History at the University of Warwick.

The relevance of this project for me came about, as even having studied French from the beginning of secondary school, I got off the Eurostar at *Gare du nord* to begin my year abroad, and had absolutely no idea where to go, what to do, what ticket to buy or any of the like to get from one side of Paris to the other. After a conversation with an SNCF representative, and a fight with the touch screen ticket machine, I had my ticket and was on my way, only to find that the ticket was in fact the wrong one, leading to a confrontation between myself, several large suitcases, and a turnstile barrier before having to purchase a second ticket to get me to where I needed to be.

This situation could easily have been avoided, and the first few weeks in Paris been made much more fluid with a little more preparation, which is why I propose the orientation exercises above

5. Taking the project forward

Discussion with Routes into Languages in July 2015 revealed some common ground between this pilot project and their Adopt a Class scheme[5]. Following consultation with the regional Adopt a Class co-ordinator based at Aston University, the next iteration of the project has incorporated features of this scheme within a particular Warwick framework, as set out below:

1. The Warwick Centre for Professional Education (CPE) (which provides PGCE training) has been engaged as a new stakeholder in the project. MFL teacher trainers at the CPE have worked with the French project leaders to identify a network of local partnership schools, both primary and secondary.

2. Nineteen participating schools, both primary and secondary, have been engaged and paired with Year Abroad students for the 2015-16 academic year.

5. See https://www.routesintolanguages.ac.uk/london/activity/2260 for more details.

3. The project now has three distinct strands:

- **The Year Abroad blog** (electronic communication between school and student via email, Powerpoint, blogs and videos).

- **The Virtual School exchange** (student ambassadors undertaking a Foreign Language Assistant role to facilitate pupil-pupil/teacher-teacher communication between French and UK schools).

- **Authentic Teaching Resources** (the collection of *realia* and development of learning activities in close collaboration with the partner school).

4. Teacher and student handbooks have been created, incorporating:

- A project agreement form tying school and student to mutually-agreed deadlines and targets.

- Template letters in French for language assistants to present to the headteachers in their overseas schools (explaining its goals and addressing issues of safeguarding).

- Sample learning activities.

5. A Moodle learning platform has been created for the exchange of resources and ideas, with dedicated areas for teacher-teacher and teacher-student dialogue, topic-based forums and video storage.

6. In consultation with the CPE, the project aims to engage MFL PGCE students within partner UK schools in resource development and analysis.

7. A project conference involving all UK stakeholders will take place in October 2016.

6. Provisional conclusions

The positive response of local schools and students to this second iteration of the project suggests the time is ripe to think about the ethics of global student exchange in more creative ways and to broaden its impact (Kehm, 2014). There is evidence to suggest that understanding of global identity grows in exchanges between mobile and non-mobile citizens:

> "The development of a global identity does not even require international study on behalf of every individual. [The University of] Malmö proposes the idea of an 'internationalisation at home', where simply by virtue of internationals visiting a foreign institution, domestic students can develop a similar identity without crossing any international borders" (Lang, 2015, p. 9)[6].

This project hopes to facilitate such encounters:

> "pupils of all backgrounds [...] will benefit from a direct connection with native speakers of the same age and the opportunity to see themselves through the eyes of another culture, thus expanding their experience as global citizens, irrespective of family background"[7].

These micro-encounters between school and university, and between home and host cultures offer innumerable possibilities for breaking down long-established boundaries. The project's personalised approach to the championing of intercultural, linguistic and social engagement will, it is hoped, provide case studies that stimulate new avenues of enquiry into affective and cognitive responses to the idea of national and international citizenship made possible by virtual and real exchanges.

---

6. Ben Lang is the student quoted earlier in the paper. His participation in the project contributed to his desire to research global student identity in further detail during his final year, see also Streitwieser (2014).

7. Georgina Newton, Senior Teaching Fellow, Warwick Centre for Professional Education; Widening Participation Development Fund application submitted Friday 3rd July 2015.

7. Acknowledgements

We would like to thank the students Ben Lang, Jack Mercer, Molly-May Blatchley-Lewis, Lauren Coates, Fiona Greig, and Gwen Venn for their participation in the project, and for granting us permission to use their names and reproduce their materials in this article.

References

Barnett, R. (2007). *A will to learn: being a student in an age of uncertainty.* Maidenhead: Open University Press.

Board, K., & Tinsley, T. (2015). *Language trends 2014/15: the state of language learning in primary and secondary schools in England.* British Council and CfBT Trust.

Freadman, A. (2014). Fragmented memory in a global age: the place of storytelling in modern language curricula. *The Modern Language Journal, 98*(1), 373-385. http://dx.doi. org/10.1111/j.1540-4781.2014.12067.x

Helle, L., Tynjälä, P., & Olkinuora, E. (2006). Project-based learning in post-secondary education – theory, practice and rubber sling shots. *Higher Education, 51*(2), 287-314.

Kehm, B. M. (2014). Beyond neo-liberalism: higher education in Europe and the global public good. In P. Gibbs & R. Barnett (Eds.), *Thinking about higher education* (pp. 91-108). NY: Springer.

Lang, B. (2015). *International student migration and the globalisation of higher education: towards the creation of a global identity?* Undergraduate dissertation, University of Warwick.

Modern Language Association Ad Hoc Committee on Foreign Languages. (2007). *Foreign languages and higher education: new structures for a changed world.* Retrieved from https://www.mla.org/Resources/Research/Surveys-Reports-and-Other-Documents/ Teaching-Enrollments-and-Programs/Foreign-Languages-and-Higher-Education-New-Structures-for-a-Changed-World

Priestland, D., Reynolds, M., Wentworth, R., Parker, M., Baker, Y., Hamnett, C., & Byrne, N. (2013, February 12). Michael Gove's new curriculum: what the experts say. *The Guardian.* Retrieved from http://www.theguardian.com/commentisfree/2013/feb/12/ round-table-draft-national-curriculum

Streitwieser, B. (Ed.) (2014). *Internationalisation of higher education and global mobility.* Oxford: Symposium Books.

13 Intercultural communicative competence: creating awareness and promoting skills in the language classroom

Sandra López-Rocha[1]

Abstract

Intercultural Communicative Competence (ICC) needs to be incorporated in the language curriculum if educators hope to help students develop an appreciation for the language and culture studied, an awareness of their own culture, and the development of skills that will allow them to be competent, adaptable, communicators. The key question addressed in this paper focuses on the importance placed on the incorporation of those skills, now recognised as crucial when learning a language: are we as teachers creating the conditions for the development of ICC, or are we simply hoping students will become interculturally competent on their own? It is, thus, necessary to understand what is meant by ICC, why must we consider fully integrating it in the language curriculum, and address the challenges associated with its inclusion.

Keywords: intercultural communicative competence, cultural awareness, language curriculum.

1. Introduction

In the last decades, *Intercultural Competence* was reintroduced as *Intercultural Communicative Competence* (ICC) as the result of its impact on foreign language teaching (López-Rocha & Arévalo-Guerrero, 2014). The distinction between the two needs to be understood when we make decisions on the cultural

1. University of Bristol, United Kingdom; S.LopezRocha@bristol.ac.uk

How to cite this chapter: López-Rocha, S. (2016). Intercultural communicative competence: creating awareness and promoting skills in the language classroom. In C. Goria, O. Speicher, & S. Stollhans (Eds), *Innovative language teaching and learning at university: enhancing participation and collaboration* (pp. 105-111). Dublin: Research-publishing.net. http://dx.doi.org/10.14705/rpnet.2016.000411

content in the curriculum. With regards to ICC, one of the key questions for language tutors is whether or not we are preparing students for this challenge: are we providing general information hoping students will develop the skills they need to communicate more efficiently and understand cultural tendencies? Or, conversely, are we creating the conditions for students to develop skills preparing them for the intercultural challenge? This paper aims, first, to address key issues in the language classroom with regards to fostering the development of ICC among foreign language students, and second, to provide practical ideas for tutors to promote ICC in a more integral way. The key idea is that students need to be further challenged and guided in order to develop critical communicative skills.

2.   Why ICC?

As Hennebry (2014) observes, "[i]t has been argued that culture is the marginalized sister of language" (p. 135). What is interesting about this quote is that this idea has been echoed by students, suggesting "[i]t would be nice if we are studying the language to know a bit more about the country and what people are like there" (Jones, 2000, p. 158). The question that remains, which is indeed our concern, is how can we help students learn about culture and develop intercultural awareness and ICC? Although it is true that we as tutors strive to provide a cultural foundation for students, this often presents important shortcomings. One of the most significant problems is that we, perhaps inadvertently, may indeed reinforce stereotypes because, instead of fostering ICC, we often focus exclusively on the language as communication, while the context in which that communication occurs, and which gives meaning to the messages, is often relegated to second place. It is, thus, necessary to understand what we mean by the culture that needs to be promoted in class. One way to visualise it is by studying the Iceberg Theory advanced by Edward T. Hall (1976), contrasting the surface/conscious (food, language, festivals) and deep/unconscious (beliefs, values, perceptions) elements of culture. These elements influence our actions, behaviours and the way we interact with each other. In addition, oftentimes these hidden elements of culture are the ones responsible for culture shock and misunderstandings, potentially leading to stereotyping and even prejudice.

It is necessary to distinguish between *Intercultural Competence* and *Intercultural Communicative Competence*. According to Byram (1997), the first refers to people's "ability to interact in their own language with the people from another country and culture," while ICC takes into account language teaching and focuses on "the ability to interact with people from another country and culture in a foreign language" (p. 71). In Byram's (1997) view, a person who has developed ICC is able to build relationships while speaking in the foreign language; communicates effectively, taking into consideration his own and the other person's viewpoint and needs; mediates interactions between people of different backgrounds, and strives to continue developing communicative skills.

3. Incorporating culture in our language classes in a different way

Globalization and migratory movements have highlighted the need to integrate interculturality in the language curriculum. This is reflected in the Council of Europe's (2001) document addressing plurilingual education in Europe in order to promote teaching and learning of signatory states' languages. This document included sections on the importance of promoting intercultural communication and the understanding of cultural differences. Other arguments supporting a more engaging role of culture in the curriculum highlight the need to explore authentic representations of culture as opposed to superficial elements; the current demand to understand identity and appreciate similarities and differences (cf. López-Rocha & Arévalo-Guerrero, 2014), our responsibility to prepare global citizens (cf. Sinicrope, Norris & Watanabe, 2007), and the result of studying other defining models, such as the US Standards for Foreign Language Learning (ACTFL, 2006) that define language goals in terms of communication, cultures, connections, comparisons, and communities, aimed at preparing students to develop linguistic and intercultural competence.

Curriculum design should take into consideration Deardorff's (2006) Process *Model of Intercultural Competence*, which emphasises the development of self-awareness, openness, and transformation (see also Furstenberg, 2010), and serves as a common denominator for various models and approaches to the development of ICC. In addition, what we should be expected to teach can be summarised in Byram's (1997; 2008) model of ICC involving five *savoirs*: knowledge, attitudes, education, skills to understand and learn.

In order to help our students become more competent in terms of culture knowledge and interactions, we should explore ready-made activities or design new ones that support objectives consistent with the development of ICC skills. With regards to their integration, we can start by observing how the CEFR incorporates culture as a component in language teaching, particularly as the classroom context is described as learner-centred, and welcomes interactivity, active participation, and cooperation among peers. Byram, Gribkova, and Starkey (2002) point out that based on the CEFR, foreign language teachers are required to promote curiosity and independent exploration and inquiry in order for students to be active participants while developing intercultural competence.

It is necessary to evaluate the materials or resources available prior to their use in our classes, as oftentimes the materials included in books may indeed be constraining or perpetuating stereotypes, instead of helping students understand diverging cultural practices. It is important for students to be further challenged and guided in order to develop critical communicative skills. Furthermore, as we strive to create the right conditions, Byram (1997) suggests that the focus should not be solely on preparing students to communicate without mistakes, but to communicate openly, forging relationships that will allow them to thrive in the foreign cultural context. We need to help students develop intercultural awareness and provide activities where the "other's" culture, values, and behaviours are considered (Byram, 1997). In order to allow students to learn about themselves and others we can use stereotypes, but only in order to deconstruct them and address misperceptions. Students will also need to first understand, and then explain, the sources of intercultural conflict and how to deal with them, while avoiding misunderstandings. Ultimately, we want to help students become interculturally competent speakers.

4.   Challenges

In addition to finding the right balance between language and culture, the types of activities we use, the level of motivation and engagement of students as well as teachers, and our own preparedness for the promotion of ICC skills, one of the greater challenges we face is assessment. It is not easy to assess the level of intercultural competence that each student has achieved, since they start with different perceptions and go through the process at different rates. It is then necessary to consider the classroom experience as a process (Byram, 1997; Deardorff, 2006), where each experience becomes the ultimate goal for each of the students. Furthermore, some researchers propose open assessment, where the student and the teacher discuss and record the progress (Scarino, 2010), while others support the idea of a portfolio, as it facilitates the interpretation of meaning, critical reflection, self-evaluation, feedback, and the opportunity to become aware of transformations (Schulz, 2007). Other challenges point at the exploration of which culture? It is not only a matter of national cultures, but also regional differences and the way the teacher's own experience and knowledge will impact the discussion.

5.   Conclusion

The need for cultural awareness continues to gather momentum, creating an urgent need to promote intercultural and linguistic competence among learners. It is our responsibility, as language teachers, to create the conditions for students to develop ICC to prepare them to interact in intercultural and diverse environments. In other words, language teaching should incorporate skills and strategies for developing cultural awareness leading to ICC for global citizenship. Culture teaching approaches should move from the descriptive to the interactionists, fostering interactions and discussion leading to self-awareness, openness, and transformation. It is necessary to be aware not only of the need to develop ICC skills, but also the challenges involved in the process. Finally, developing intercultural awareness must be combined with language learning, where we use our own experience to enhance the students' exploration of culture: Their own and that of the target language.

References

ACTFL. (2006). *Standards for foreign language learning in the 21st century.* Yonkers, NY: National Standards in Foreign Language Education Project.

Byram, M. (1997). *Teaching and assessing intercultural communicative competence.* Clevendon: Multilingual Matters.

Byram, M. (2008). *From foreign language education to education for intercultural citizenship: essays and reflections.* Clevendon: Multilingual Matters.

Byram, M., Gribkova, B., & Starkey, H. (2002). *Developing the intercultural dimension in language teaching: a practical introduction for teachers.* Strasbourg: Council of Europe.

Council of Europe. (2001). *Common European framework of reference for languages.* Cambridge: University Press.

Deardorff, D. K. (2006). Identification and assessment of intercultural competence as a student outcome of internationalization. *Journal Studies in International Education, 10*(3), 241-266. http://dx.doi.org/10.1177/1028315306287002

Furstenberg, G. (2010). Making culture the core of the language class: Can it be done? *The Modern Language Journal, 94*(2), 329-332. http://dx.doi.org/10.1111/j.1540-4781.2010.01027.x

Hall, E. T. (1976). *Beyond culture.* New York: Anchor.

Hennebry, M. (2014). Cultural awareness: should it be taught? Can it be taught? In P. Driscoll, E. Macaro, & A. Swerbrick (Eds.), *Debates in modern languages education.* London: Routledge.

Jones, B. (2000). Developing cultural awareness. In K. Field (Ed.), *Issues in modern foreign languages teaching.* London: RoutledgeFalmer.

López-Rocha, S., & Arévalo-Guerrero, E. (2014). Intercultural communication discourse. In M. Lacorte (Ed.), *The Routledge handbook of Hispanic applied linguistics.* New York: Routledge.

Scarino, A. (2010). Assessing intercultural capability in learning languages: a renewed understanding of language, culture, learning, and the nature of assessment. *The Modern Language Journal, 94*(2), 324-329. http://dx.doi.org/10.1111/j.1540-4781.2010.01026.x

Sinicrope, C., Norris, J. M., & Watanabe, Y. (2007). Understanding and assessing intercultural competence: a summary of theory, research, and practice. *Second Language Studies, 26*(1), 1-58.

Schulz, R. A. (2007). The challenge of assessing cultural understanding in the context of foreign language instruction. *Foreign Language Annals, 40*(1), 9-26. http://dx.doi.org/10.1111/j.1944-9720.2007.tb02851.x

14 Anything can happen out there: a holistic approach to field trips

Alessia Plutino[1]

Abstract

This paper looks back at an academic-led language field trip project, now in its third year, involving ab-initio students of Italian at the University of Southampton. It considers the role of academic-led field trips in Modern Languages (ML) and it explores the underlying pedagogical approaches that were adopted to enhance students' engagement, participation and collaboration during the trips and beyond. It also investigates the opportunities that Web 2.0 brought to teachers and learners and how these were adapted for a field trip where technology and social media make learning more inclusive and engaging. The project also sought to develop students' employability skills by introducing the role of the 'student-assistant' working closely with the academic in charge of the trip. The paper will describe the robust pedagogical reflective process employed during the project and how it influenced project design. It will conclude by suggesting that ML departments would benefit from innovative approaches in field trips.

Keywords: trip abroad, ab-initio language learning, cultural awareness, Web 2.0, social media, student employability.

1. University of Southampton; United Kingdom; a.plutino@soton.ac.uk

How to cite this chapter: Plutino, A. (2016). Anything can happen out there: a holistic approach to field trips. In C. Goria, O. Speicher, & S. Stollhans (Eds), *Innovative language teaching and learning at university: enhancing participation and collaboration* (pp. 113-120). Dublin: Research-publishing.net. http://dx.doi.org/10.14705/rpnet.2016.000412

1. Introduction

Field trips run by academics with the aim to expand and deepen learning outside the classroom environment have been used in many disciplines at all levels in education.

At university level, the attitude towards them is of a mixed nature, with funding issues as well as administrative workloads having a negative impact.

There is evidence that field trip outcomes result in both cognitive and non-cognitive learning (for a review see Dewitt & Storksdieck, 2008) and research has also shown that:

- exposure to a variety of new contexts and experiences allows field trips to become a way to widen students' interest and engagement (Bonderup Dohn, 2011; Kisiel, 2005);

- field trip dynamics enable a more positive student's attitude towards the subject (Csikszentmihalyi & Hermanson, 1995; Nadelson & Jordan, 2012);

- they are formative experiences with both short and long-term outcomes (Falk & Dierking, 1997; Salmi, 2003; Wolins, Jensen, & Ulzheimer, 1992).

In ML, however, field trips appear to be in decline as there are many independent opportunities to practice a foreign language abroad without the need of an accompanying tutor. The growing importance of intercultural understanding means that more guided and structured tasks are needed in order to fulfil cultural understanding and integrate it into language learning.

In this paper, through a short case study within ML, I will look into the value and the benefits of academic-led field trips for both learners and leading academic staff in this specific discipline. In particular, I will focus on whether or not field trips can enhance students' engagement, participation and collaboration amongst all participants, academic staff included. To discuss this, I will use evidence gathered during a three-year project.

2. Background

I teach an Italian language Accelerated 1+2 course, an ab-initio course devoted to able linguists who already have one or two foreign languages at intermediate level. This is a fast paced course and students complete two years in one.

In 2013 I arranged a first informal field trip for a small group of students. This took place during the Easter break and we visited a small town in Le Marche.

I gathered strong evidence on the learners' enthusiasm and sense of achievement as well as their spontaneous wish to share experiences with fellow students who could not join the trip. I therefore started to investigate and evaluate some teaching and learning theories which could support a more collaborative and networked acquisition of knowledge to be adopted in future field trips.

My intention, as a proactive user of technology for teaching myself, was to integrate and make the most out of Web 2.0 opportunities.

3. Implementation of a pilot scheme

In 2014, an analysis of students' course evaluation feedback highlighted a lack of opportunities to experience Italian culture, lifestyle and everyday life, the knowledge of which is required to fulfil the intercultural aspect of such a fast paced language course. A trip to Italy was becoming a recurrent request on feedback forms. I therefore decided to give the trip a more formal structure, taking into consideration specific advice emerged from research into the field (Stronck, 1983).

The research shows several things: guidance and support received during field trips enable students to investigate in a more personal and relevant manner, avoiding an overly rigid classroom instruction approach (Griffin & Symington, 1997; Jensen 1994). It also emerges that students who are left to face the challenges of field trips without appropriate preparation, might experience a negative learning outcome (Orion & Hofstein, 1994).

DeWitt and Osborne (2007) emphasise the core concept of 'joint productive activities', as "the purpose is to motivate students' discussions with each other and an adult facilitator using their personal interests and curiosity as a starting point" (p. 690).

I successfully applied to the University of Southampton 'Student Opportunity Fund' and set up a pilot scheme aimed at the development of a sustainable and replicable framework for a ML field trip. Its name, 'Italy DIY', underlined the importance of students actively engaging in their own learning.

The main features of the scheme were that:

- students would visit places and engage in practical activities (experiential learning; Kolb, 1984);

- students would focus on a particular aspect in which they are interested (curiosity, independent learning).

Other important aspects were that students should:

- observe, discuss, reflect, compare, share knowledge (dialogic learning: collective, supportive, reciprocal, cumulative, purposeful; Alexander, 2010);

- students design content/resources (oral/written/video) for sharing their experiences and interests (as open resources, or via social media: use of technology, networked learners);

- implement a trip blog (www.blog.soton.ac.uk/italydiy) and develop digital literacy;

- develop and publish Open Educational Resources to form a growing repository of learning and teaching materials that could inform future trips.

In terms of students' autonomy, the pilot scheme aimed at:

- developing multidisciplinary independent learning and engagement with authentic topics and resources;

- implementing the Student Assistant role (appointed via a formal job interview, all trip expenses paid).

The Student Assistant role would allow a student of Italian with a higher level of spoken and written language, to plan the trip in collaboration and under the guidance of the leading academic. They would be involved in a series of activities before, during and after the trip, thus enhancing their employability skills by acquiring organization, decision-making and planning skills, and by taking risks and working in a team. The ideal Student Assistant has an interest in teaching as he/she will co-lead activities to improve group understanding of cultural issues as well as facilitating language related tasks.

4.   Outcomes of the pilot scheme

As a result of the pilot scheme, the learning and teaching outcomes of the 2014 field trip were more structured and tangible. For example, students had to produce collaborative projects in the target language at the end of the trip and a reflective piece in English on the experience. Having been exposed to a vast amount of stimuli, students produced projects which were extremely diverse in nature and included a variety of topics, covering areas such as art, religion, history, architecture, local food, etc.

Students used a variety of tools and formats (writing, video, etc) to produce their projects, showing their own individuality and creativity. The leading academic's and Student Assistant's task was to foster collaboration during experiential learning (new role of educator=guide, co-investigator) and at the same time find strategies for learners to engage directly with the rich environment so that they could take charge of their own development (holistic education; Miller, 2004). In such a way, learners' interests were activated by curiosity for the new environment/culture (Networked learners). The trip blog served as a learning and teaching platform and also acted as a dissemination tool as students began to act as 'ambassadors', running sessions about their experience at various in-house events.

5.   Evaluation

The analysis of learners' feedback and reflective writing so far has shown new ways in which learners and academics can interact in dynamic learning communities. A more spontaneous teaching and learning experience fosters students' engagement and enhances learning and teaching by providing multiple learning modalities in which learners' interests can develop and flourish. As a result, learners rediscover their own discipline but more importantly, embrace interdisciplinary areas.

My personal gain, as leading academic staff, has been to rediscover my own country and culture through my students' eyes. The questions they ask about what they experience in situ helps me reflect upon my own biases and insider/outsider paradoxes, informing my future teaching.

6.   Conclusion

There is need to do further research into the benefits and most effective implementations of field trips in ML, but this can only be done if tutors start thinking 'outside classroom walls'.

The project has shown that if leading academic staff uses their expertise to suggest learning paths in the world at large according to learners' preferences, then truly, 'anything can happen out there'.

The ML department at Southampton was so pleased with the outcomes of the pilot project that in 2015 they agreed to subsidise an extra week-long language course following the field trip.

Future developments include the Student Assistant taking a more leading role and eventually become in charge of trip activities and extending the scheme to other languages in ML.

References

Alexander, R. J. (2010). *Dialogic teaching essentials.* University of Cambridge. Retrieved from http://scholars.nie.edu.sg/files/oer/FINAL%20Dialogic%20Teaching%20Essentials.pdf

Bonderup Dohn, N. (2011). Situational interest of high school students who visit an aquarium. *Science Education, 95*(2), 337-357. http://dx.doi.org/10.1002/sce.20425

Csikszentmihalyi, M., & Hermanson, K. (1995). Intrinsic motivation in museums: why does one want to learn? In J. H. Falk & L. D. Dierking (Eds.), *Public institutions for personal learning* (pp. 67-77). Washington, DC: American Association of Museums.

DeWitt, J., & Osborne J. (2007). Supporting teachers on science-focused school trips: Towards an integrated framework of theory and practice. *International Journal of Science Education, 29*(6), 685-710. http://dx.doi.org/10.1080/09500690600802254

Dewitt, J., & Storksdieck, M. (2008). A short review of school field trips: key findings from the past and implications for the future. *Visitor Studies, 11*(2), 181-197. http://dx.doi.org/10.1080/10645570802355562

Falk, J. H., & Dierking, L. D. (1997). School field trips: assessing their long-term impact. *Curator: The Museum Journal, 40*(3), 211-218. http://dx.doi.org/10.1111/j.2151-6952.1997.tb01304.x

Griffin, J., & Symington, D. (1997). Moving from task-oriented to learning-oriented strategies on school excursions to museums. *Science Education, 81*(6), 763-779.

Jensen, N. (1994). Children's perceptions of their museum experiences: a contextual perspective. *Children's Environments, 11*(4), 300-324.

Kisiel, J. F. (2005). Understanding elementary teacher motivations for science fieldtrips. *Science Education, 89*(6), 936-955, http://dx.doi.org/10.1002/sce.20085

Kolb, D. A. (1984). *Experiential learning: experience as the source of learning and development.* New Jersey: Prentice-Hall Inc.

Miller, R. (2004). Educational alternatives: a map of the territory. *Paths of Learning, 20,* 20-27.

Nadelson, L., & Jordan, R. (2012). Student attitudes toward and recall of outside day: an environmental science field trip. *The Journal of Educational Research, 105*(3), 220-231. http://dx.doi.org/10.1080/00220671.2011.576715

Orion, N., & Hofstein, A. (1994). Factors that influence learning during a scientific field trip in a natural environment. *Journal of Research in Science Teaching, 31*(10), 1097-1119. http://dx.doi.org/10.1002/tea.3660311005

Salmi, H. (2003). Science centres as learning laboratories: experiences of Heureka, the Finnish Science Centre. *International Journal of Technology Management, 25*(5), 460-476. http://dx.doi.org/10.1504/IJTM.2003.003113

Stronck, D. R. (1983). The comparative effects of different museum tours on children's attitudes and learning. *Journal of Research in Science Teaching, 20*(4), 283-290. http://dx.doi.org/10.1002/tea.3660200403

Wolins, I. S., Jensen, N., & Ulzheimer, R. (1992). Children's memories of museum field trips: a qualitative study. *Journal of Museum Education, 17*(2), 17-27. Retrieved from: http://www.jstor.org/stable/40478925

15 The dichotomy of language and content in US and UK higher education – Implications for the development of intercultural competence and perspectives towards the target language

Elinor Parks[1]

Abstract

The complex relationship between language and culture has been widely problematised in applied linguistics and education (see Byram, 1997; Byrnes, 2002; Kramsch, 1993; Risager, 2006). While this issue has been extensively explored from a theoretical perspective, few studies have examined the complexity of this relationship from the curricular/structural approach towards Modern Language degrees. The American Modern Language Association (MLA, 2007) report, as well as reports issued in the UK such as the Worton (2009) report, similarly refer to a division in the content and language elements of the degree and advocate for a curricular reform in which a more integrative approach is adopted for languages in higher education. The paper reports on some of the initial findings from a Ph.D. study exploring the implications of dualistic approaches towards language and content on the student experience and more specifically on the place of the target language and the development of intercultural competence. The results reported are drawn from student questionnaires and follow-up interviews from two American and two English universities.

Keywords: language degrees, content, higher education, target language, culture, intercultural competence.

1. University of Hull/Leeds Beckett University, United Kingdom; e.parks@2013.hull.ac.uk

How to cite this chapter: Parks, E. (2016). The dichotomy of language and content in US and UK higher education – Implications for the development of intercultural competence and perspectives towards the target language. In C. Goria, O. Speicher, & S. Stollhans (Eds), *Innovative language teaching and learning at university: enhancing participation and collaboration* (pp. 121-129). Dublin: Research-publishing.net. http://dx.doi.org/10.14705/rpnet.2016.000413

1. Introduction

The study explores the complex relationship of the separation between language and content and its implications for the student experience in higher education. It is situated in a context of uncertainty for the future of language degrees. While the decline in uptake at secondary level remains a concern at secondary level (Worton, 2009), as Gallagher-Brett and Broady (2012) argue, "the sense of crisis appears to be particularly marked in higher education" (p. 263).

In light of the concerning status of Modern Languages as a discipline in the UK, some studies (see Busse & Walter, 2013; Gieve & Cunico, 2012) have problematised the traditional separation between language and content still very much present in many Russell Group and older universities, which now teach the majority of Modern Language degree students in the country (Kelly, 2013).

Among other issues, the curricular separation brings into question the place of the target language and its relationship with the target culture. It also raises questions with regards to establishing relevant links between the two elements of the curriculum. As Brumfit et al. (2005) argue, "consideration of the exact nature of the interaction between language and content is often neglected" (p. 158). While in the USA Modern Language curricula differ considerably, the literature identifies a similar problematic relationship between language and content.

It refers to a 'bifurcation' between lower-level language courses on one end and upper-level literature and culture courses on the other (Paesani & Allen, 2012), often resulting in a difficult transition for students from lower to upper level (Maxim, 2006). In this regard, the MLA (2007) report argues that "a two-tiered structure impedes the development of a unified curriculum" (pp. 2-3), and suggests that "a curriculum should consist of a series of complementary or linked courses that holistically incorporate content and cross-cultural reflection at every level" (p. 5). The document also places emphasis on the objectives of a ML degree and argues that "the language major should be structured to produce a specific outcome: educated speakers who have deep translingual and transcultural competence" (MLA, 2007, p. 3). This is similarly voiced in the Worton (2009) report, which argues that "universities should take a more active leadership role [...] by emphasising the importance of intercultural competence and multi-lingual skills" (p. 35).

The paper hence examines student perspectives, in both contexts, on being taught in the target language and perceived opportunities to develop intercultural competence.

The study adopts Byram's (1997) model for intercultural competence and places particular emphasis on his fifth savoir, critical cultural awareness[2], which, as he argues is "the crucial educational dimension of intercultural competence" (Byram, 2009, p. 326).

2. Method

2.1. Settings and participants

The research reported in this paper is drawn from an ongoing Ph.D. project. The study employed a mixed-methods approach comprising of questionnaire surveys and follow-up interviews. Data was collected from students enrolled on a German degree programme in four universities. The institutions taking part were assigned a pseudonym to ensure confidentiality of the responses. University A and University B are both located in northern England. University A follows a traditional curriculum, where language is taught alongside content. All content teaching takes place in English. The curriculum at University B, on the other hand, demonstrates an evident effort to increase relevance through content taught for the most part in German and a more text-based approach towards the teaching of language. With regards to

---

2. "An ability to evaluate, critically and on the basis of explicit criteria, perspectives, practices and products in one's own and other cultures and countries" (Byram, 1997, p. 53).

the US institutions, University C is a very well established university located on the East Coast. Its German department has been specifically redesigned to adopt a genre-based content-oriented curriculum throughout the degree programme and hence provides an example of an alternative to what has been identified in the literature as a two-tiered structure. University D, located on the West Coast, to an extent reflects a two-tiered structure, although a number of courses fall into a middle area between a lower-level language course and upper-level content course.

2.2.   Data collection

The data collection took place over the period of 10 weeks; it commenced with the questionnaire survey (using a 6 point Likert scale ranging from 1=strongly disagree to 6=strongly agree) and was followed by semi-structured interviews with students willing to take part.

The paper reviews some of these results in light of the issues raised in the literature and proposes some pedagogical recommendations based on the findings.

3.   Discussion and conclusions

Results from the questionnaire illustrate the different student attitudes towards being taught content in the TL and students' perception of their programme as more or less integrated. The results (see Figure 1) show that students in programmes where the main medium of instruction for content modules was not German (University A - UK), or where some content was taught in German and some in English (University D - USA), felt that language and content should be better integrated.

There was a negative correlation between the two variables (see Table 1) indicating that the more content is taught in the TL, the less students feel that language and content should be better integrated in their programme. The data seem to indicate that, from a student perspective, a higher proportion of TL used across the curriculum can be regarded as one of the characteristics of more integrated programmes.

Figure 1. Students' perceptions on integration of language and content

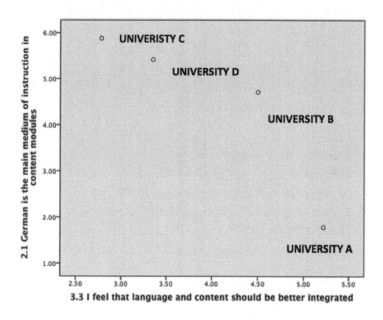

3.3 I feel that language and content should be better integrated

Table 1. Correlation test

		2.1 German is the main medium of instruction in content modules	3.3 I feel that language and content should be better integrated
2.1 German is the main medium of instruction in content modules	Pearson Correlation	1	-.903*
	Sig. (1-tailed)		.048
	N	4	4
3.3 I feel that language and content should be better integrated	Pearson Correlation	-903*	1
	Sig. (1-tailed)	.048	
	N	4	4

*Correlation is significant at the 0.05 level (1-tailed).

With regards to the implications of the different curricula on the development of intercultural competence, the more insightful findings were drawn from the qualitative analysis of student interviews. The questionnaire results, however, did highlight a difference in overall mean scores obtained from the multi-item scale for the fifth savoir: critical cultural awareness (see Table 2).

Table 2.   Mean values for critical cultural awareness

University A	University B	University C	University D
4.78	4.92	5.09	5.04

University C, with the highest rating, was also the institution with greatest integration between language and content.

Furthermore, there was a significant difference between mean scores for critical cultural awareness and similarity in feedback and relevance between language and content ($p<0.04$), suggesting a possible relationship between certain curricular approaches and students' perceived opportunities to develop critical cultural awareness.

While scores for intercultural competence were slightly lower in the two UK universities, evidence of how this was developed through the learning experience was voiced in interviews. Zak from University A, for instance, referred to the unique contribution of content modules,

"The modern women writers module made me think about social conditioning and how history... how religion plays a part in bringing somebody up into the world and the views they form. You've got to look at this from a Russian person's point of view".

In this statement the student demonstrated a clear understanding of what Byram (1997) defines as critical cultural awareness as he was able to identify how elements which influence the establishment of cultural beliefs, such as history and religion, shape views and perspectives on other cultures and countries. While at University A students referred to specific content modules, at University C, the reference extended to the overall learning experience. One of the students interviewed was particularly articulate in describing how the university experience had transformed his world views and enabled him to make comparisons between his home culture and the target culture.

"East Germany has a lot of the same problems […] that we do, you think about both sides and how you fit in where. And what happens when you place yourself in that society, what would I be like if I were East German, what would life be like? […] And I think… in doing that you come to the conclusion about how you fit in".

The results of the study would appear to indicate that programmes which strive to integrate the language and content elements of the degree are better able to extend opportunities for a critical engagement with culture beyond specific content modules. In institutions where language was taught separately from content, students generally referred to the critical dimension most often in reference to their content modules, in line with Mitchell et al. (2004) who found that in "interviews both tutors and students talk most about critical thinking and engaging with the world when discussing content rather than language classes" (cited in Brumfit et al., 2005, p. 159).

Three recommendations for higher education are made based on the initial findings: firstly, to recognise the invaluable contribution of content modules for the development of the critical dimension, secondly to consider how the language modules may similarly contribute to this development and thirdly to reflect upon the role of the target language in bridging the language and content curricula in order to achieve a more holistic curriculum.

4.   Acknowledgements

I would like to acknowledge the strong support received by the School of Languages, Linguistics and Cultures at the University of Hull as well as the warm welcome received by all participating institutions, whose support was invaluable for this project.

References

Brumfit, C., Myles, F., Mitchell, R., Johnston, B., & Ford, P. (2005). Language study in higher education and the development of criticality. *International Journal of Applied Linguistics,* 15(2), 145-168. http://dx.doi.org/10.1111/j.1473-4192.2005.00085.x

Busse, V., & Walter, C. (2013). Foreign language learning motivation in higher education: a longitudinal study of motivational changes and their causes. *The Modern Language Journal, 97*(2), 1-22. http://dx.doi.org/10.1111/j.1540-4781.2013.12004.x

Byram, M. (1997). *Teaching and assessing intercultural communicative competence.* Clevedon: Multilingual Matters.

Byram, M. (2009). Intercultural competence in foreign languages: the intercultural speaker and the pedagogy of foreign language education. In D. K. Deardoff (Ed.), *The SAGE handbook of intercultural competence.* Thousand Oaks, CA: Sage.

Byrnes, H. (2002). The cultural turn in foreign language departments: challenge and opportunity. *Profession,* 114-129. http://dx.doi.org/10.1632/074069502X85176

Gallagher-Brett, A., & Broady, E. (2012). Teaching languages in higher education. *The Language Learning Journal, 40*(3), 263-271. http://dx.doi.org/10.1080/09571736.2012.723938

Gieve, S., & Cunico, S. (2012). Language and content in the modern foreign languages degree: a students' perspective. *The Language Learning Journal, 40*(3), 273-291. http://dx.doi.org/10.1080/09571736.2011.639459

Kelly, M. (2013). The future of language degrees: report of CEL/ELC special interest group. *European Journal of Language Policy, 5*(1), 139-153.

Kramsch, C. (1993). *Context and culture in language teaching.* Oxford: Oxford University Press.

Maxim, H. (2006). Integrating textual thinking into the introductory college-level foreign language classroom. *The Modern Language Journal, 90*(1), 19-32. http://dx.doi.org/10.1111/j.1540-4781.2006.00382.x

Mitchell, R., Johnston, B., Ford, P., Brumfit, C., & Myles, F. (2004). *The contribution of residence abroad to student critical development.* Paper presented at the BERA Annual Conference, September.

MLA. (2007). *Foreign languages and higher education: new structures for a changed world.* Retrieved from http://www.mla.org/flreport

Paesani, K., & Allen, H. W. (2012). Beyond the language-content divide: research on advanced foreign language instruction at the postsecondary level. *Foreign Language Annals, 45*(s1), s54-s75. http://dx.doi.org/10.1111/j.1944-9720.2012.01179.x

Risager, K. (2006). *Language and culture: global flows and local complexity.* Clevedon, UK: Multilingual Matters.

Worton, M. (2009). *Review of modern languages provision in higher education in England.* London, UK: HEFCE Issues paper 2009/41.

16 We're all language teachers now: teaching subject discipline content through the medium of a second language

Neil Hughes[1]

Abstract

This paper looks at the teaching of subject discipline content through the medium of a second language. It begins by looking at the globalisation of discipline content teaching through second languages, whereby increasing numbers of academics and students are either teaching or learning in universities across the globe in a language other than their mother tongue. It then looks at the ways in which questions about the language of subject content delivery are being addressed by departments of languages in UK universities. The paper argues that practice is differentiated along up to 3 main and several sub-dimensions of both comprehension and communication. The third section sets out some of the research evidence into the effectiveness of subject content teaching in the target language, in particular, for developing students' academic writing skills. It concludes with recommendations about the future direction of language and content teaching in the UK.

Keywords: globalisation, target language, content, academic writing.

1. University of Nottingham, Nottingham, United Kingdom; neil.hughes@nottingham.ac.uk

How to cite this chapter: Hughes, N. (2016). We're all language teachers now: teaching subject discipline content through the medium of a second language. In C. Goria, O. Speicher, & S. Stollhans (Eds), *Innovative language teaching and learning at university: enhancing participation and collaboration* (pp. 131-137). Dublin: Research-publishing.net. http://dx.doi.org/10.14705/rpnet.2016.000414

1. The globalisation of discipline content teaching through second languages

Teaching and learning discipline content through a second language is an increasingly common feature of the global Higher Education (HE) scene. Europe, for example, has seen a significant increase in this practice as universities across the region have shifted delivery from their official national language to English. The main driver of this development is a process of global market formation in HE. Thus, as national barriers to the marketing of education services have been eroded, the study destination choices of those with the necessary qualifications and economic resources have increased. As competition from English-speaking countries has grown, universities in non-English speaking countries have been compelled to provide courses in the global lingua-franca as they struggle to both retain their best home students and provide them with the skills they need to compete in the global marketplace. This is a theme addressed by Dickson (2009), who argues that in the context of globalisation, universities are under pressure from national governments to provide the highly educated workforce equipped with the skills, including foreign language proficiency, necessary in the global knowledge economy. There are of course, also financial pressures. As Fortanet-Gómez (2013) explains, universities are being urged to cut costs and boost income by increasing recruitment of fee-paying English L1 and L2 students from around the world.

For universities in the UK, the global HE market is seen as an opportunity to increase income in a challenging funding environment in which the burden for financing HE is shifting inexorably from the state to students. Given that international students pay as much as three times more than home students for a university place in the UK, it is unsurprising that universities have sought to increase recruitment from abroad. According to the UCAS website (2015), there are currently over 400, 000 international students in the UK studying subjects in what for many of them will be a second language. The majority of these students are located in London, where in some institutions, the number of international students exceeds that of home students. For example, whilst at the London

School of Economics, 67% of its students are described as international, at the London Business School more than 7 out of 10 students are from overseas.

Given the extent of this change, it must be of some concern that little consideration appears to be given to the pedagogical implications of teaching large numbers of students through a language, English, that most have learnt as a foreign language at schools or in other contexts. As Fürstenberg and Kletzenbauer (2015) point out, in the Austrian case, many of the teachers involved are non-native English speaking content teachers with little preparation and support from their institutions. As a consequence,

> "there is often little awareness of the complexity of teaching and learning through an additional language. Not only are the challenges of this situation not addressed, the potential for this situation for integrating content and language learning is sadly not realized either" (Fürstenberg & Kletzenbauer, 2015, p. 2).

2. Content and language integrated teaching in UK departments of languages

One area of HE where the question of how best to teach content knowledge to non-native speakers has attracted attention is in the UK's many and varied departments of languages. Anecdotal evidence and personal experience suggest that the ways in which academics located within them address subject content delivery is as eclectic and diverse as the cultural and societal knowledge taught on their programmes. Regarding the language of delivery, for example, instead of in terms of an antagonistic binary (either English or the target language), academics located in these departments approach this issue in a more complex and nuanced way that takes into account various dimensions of delivery, including, but not restricted to, the language used in the classroom.

To understand the range of approaches employed, I argue that it is helpful to think in terms of three main dimensions of language comprehension and communication: input, output and social interaction; and several sub-dimensions including teacher talk, written, audio and audio-visual textual input, essay writing, oral output and face-to-face and computer-mediated social interaction. In each case, it is useful to think of a continuum ranging from 100% exclusively in English to 100% exclusively in the target language (see Figure 1).

Figure 1.   Communication and comprehension continuum

Output

English 100%------------------Input: Reading------------------------	**TL 100%**
English 100%------------------Input: Listening-----------------------	**TL 100%**

Input

English 100%------------------Interaction: Speaking-----------------	**TL 100%**
English 100%------------------Interaction: Writing-------------------	**TL 100%**

Social Interaction

English 100%------------------Output: Writing---------------------	**TL 100%**
English 100%------------------Output: Speaking---------------------	**TL 100%**

In order to illustrate how academics approach these dimensions it is helpful to imagine two hypothetical teacher typologies. These are conceptually rather than empirically derived types that are used here heuristically to help investigate and make recommendations about practice. Type 1 is the academic that believes that classroom use of the target language is an impediment to the intellectual exchange between academics and students. As a consequence, his/her position is firmly to the left in every dimension. Type 2 on the other hand, is less sceptical about comprehensibility and convinced of the language learning benefits of target language delivery. His/her practice is more likely to be located to the right of the dimensions.

The reality on the ground in language departments is that a much more eclectic range of practices exists than these typologies suggest. Thus, in the case of academics delivering their cultural and/or social content through the medium of English, it is likely that at least some, if not all, of the primary texts will be read in the original language of publication. If we take an example from my own teaching, a Latin-American Studies module delivered at Nottingham Trent University to second year post A-level students studying Spanish on a joint-honours programme, the approach might be more usefully described as hybrid. As Figure 2 suggests, whilst some of the sub-dimensions (teacher talk) were delivered almost exclusively in the target language, others were located elsewhere on their relevant continuum. In the case of reading input, for example, students were exposed to a range of texts both in English and the target language.

Figure 2. Hybrid approach

Dimension 1
English 60%------------------Input: Reading------------------------ **TL 40%**
English 10%------------------Input: Listening------------------ **TL 90%**

Dimension 2
English 0%------------------Interaction: Speaking----------------- **TL 100%**
English 0%------------------Interaction: Writing-------------------- **TL 100%**

Dimension 3
English 80%------------------Output: Writing--------------------- **TL 20%**
English 0%------------------Output: Speaking---------------------- **TL 100%**

3.   Impact of target language delivery

What then of the language learning impact of teaching cultural and societal content through the medium of the target language? My own research suggests that there are very important benefits ensuing from this approach, particularly in the area of students' acquisition of academic writing skills. This is an issue I discuss in a paper published in the Latin-American Content and Language

Integrated Journal (Hughes, 2013). In it, I assess the development of academic writing skills amongst students taking a final year undergraduate module in Latin American Studies.

The paper demonstrates, through discourse analysis of student contributions to an online discussion forum, how through exposure to discipline content in the target language and regular opportunities to practice academic writing, students develop the capacity to communicate information in a discipline specific way using many of the lexico-grammatical features commonly found in Spanish academic writing such as discipline-related technical terms, use of the passive *se*, impersonal statements, cual clauses, and nominalisation:

> "The paper provides evidence of students' proficiency in the productive use of complex academic-prose in a teaching and learning context lacking an explicit focus on form. Like Kern (2000), it identifies the key variables in the development of students' academic writing as regular access to authentic academic discourse in the subject area and sustained opportunities to practice writing about syllabus content. It also, like Kern (2000), emphasises the importance of discussion and debate and the role new technologies can play in stimulating this. This framework is proving sufficient to ensure that the academic language (as well as the content, and critical thinking) goals of the module are being achieved" (Hughes, 2013, p. 44).

4.   Conclusions

In this paper, I have discussed the issue of subject content teaching through a second language. In it, I have shown that regardless of discipline, many institutions across the globe require their academics to teach in languages (primarily English) other than their mother tongue. I have also demonstrated that despite its rapid increase, little thought has been given to the many pedagogical challenges posed by teaching discipline content through a second language to mixed cohorts of home and international students with very different levels of proficiency in the language of instruction. If universities are to develop a more systematic approach to the needs of these teachers and learners, they could do worse than draw on expertise residing in language departments, where strategies for making input comprehensible, providing opportunities for social interaction and communicating meaning through speaking and writing are standard features of the pedagogical toolkit.

Finally, I suggest that those academics delivering cultural and social content in language departments in the UK might also give some thought to the input, output, social interaction profiles of the modules they teach. Although they might still conclude that their content is too complex for classes to be delivered in the target language, such consideration might reveal other ways to integrate exposure and use of the relevant L2 into their pedagogical mix.

References

Dickson, T. (2009). Knowledge transfer and the globalisation of higher education. *Journal of Knowledge-based Innovation in China, 1*(3), 174-184. http://dx.doi.org/10.1108/17561410910990566

Fortanet-Gómez, I. (2013). *CLIL in higher education: towards a multilingual language Policy*. Bristol, UK: Multilingual Matters.

Fürstenberg, & Kletzenbauer, P (2015). Language-sensitive CLIL teaching in higher education: approaches to successful lesson planning. *ELTWorldOnline.com, Special Issue on CLIL*. Retrieved from http://blog.nus.edu.sg/eltwo/?p=4791

Hughes, N. (2013). Developing academic register in CLIL: an exploratory study of Spanish L2 students' Latin American political economy writing in the UK. *Latin American Journal of Content and Language Integrated Learning, 6*(2), 42-71. http://dx.doi.org/10.5294/laclil.2013.6.2.3

Kern, R. (2000). *Literacy and language teaching*. Oxford, UK: Oxford University Press.

UCAS (2015). *International and EU students*. Retrieved from https://www.ucas.com/ucas/undergraduate/getting-started/international-and-eu-students

17 Challenges faced by Cantonese speakers in a UK university Mandarin course

Lan Lo[1]

Abstract

After Hong Kong returned to China in 1997, those in the Chinese migrant community in the UK who anticipated returning to China saw the significant benefits of learning Mandarin. The challenges are not only related to the social and cultural differences between the Cantonese and Mandarin migrant groups, but also the intrinsic linguistic differences between the two languages. This case study investigated students' motivation, needs and barriers in relation to Chinese Mandarin learning. Previous research (Lo & Chen, 2014) found there was a communication gap between Cantonese and Mandarin speakers within the Chinese migrant community. This gap poses difficulties to the Cantonese speakers in their Chinese Mandarin learning. Establishing a Languages Exchanges Community (LEC) programme, involving both Cantonese and Mandarin groups, is seen as an appropriate means to bridge the gap and increase the learning outcomes for Cantonese speakers.

Keywords: Cantonese speakers, Chinese Mandarin learning, Chinese migrant community, languages exchange community.

1. University of Nottingham, Nottingham, United Kingdom; lan.lo@nottingham.ac.uk

How to cite this chapter: Lo, L. (2016). Challenges faced by Cantonese speakers in a UK university Mandarin course. In C. Goria, O. Speicher, & S. Stollhans (Eds), *Innovative language teaching and learning at university: enhancing participation and collaboration* (pp. 139-145). Dublin: Research-publishing.net. http://dx.doi.org/10.14705/rpnet.2016.000415

1. Introduction

With China's rise in influence, the teaching of Chinese as a heritage/community language has emerged as a key issue in the Chinese diaspora of Europe (Lo, 2014). According to Shum, Tsung and Gao (2011), Hong Kong's reintegration with China has raised both the value and use of Putonghua (Chinese Mandarin) in Hong Kong. It has been speculated that more and more Cantonese speakers started to learn Chinese Mandarin in order to understand more about the contemporary mainland of China in terms of social, economic and cultural aspects. However, in relation to the significance of learning Chinese Mandarin, there is little research highlighting the needs and challenges faced by Cantonese speakers.

Although Mandarin and Cantonese share a similar writing system (Cantonese speakers use the traditional version of Chinese characters while Mandarin speakers from Mainland China use a simplified version), hundreds of Cantonese colloquial characters are either completely unrecognizable or with unpredictable different meanings; there are also differences regarding phonetic and phonological aspects between the two languages.

In the above context, this paper reflects the needs and barriers of Cantonese speakers in a university course, and using West's (1994) needs analysis approach, the objective was to identify what learners will be required to do with the foreign language in the target situation, and how learners might best master the target language during the period of training. The research was designed to explore the following questions:

- What are the reasons which motivate Cantonese speakers to learn Chinese Mandarin?

- What teaching approach works best for them?

- What barriers are they facing during the learning and what are their reasons?

- What factors can help them to overcome the barriers and improve their learning outcomes?

The case study describes the different methods for data collection, which aimed to understand learners' needs and barriers, and explores a productive way of Mandarin education for the Cantonese speakers within the Chinese migrant community.

2.   The case study

The case study was carried out on a 'Mandarin for Cantonese speakers' module at the University of Nottingham from September 2012 to March 2014. In this study, classroom observation, questionnaires and in-depth interviews were employed; a total of 150 hours was observed and 119 questionnaires were received.

The gender breakdown of the learner respondents is 25% male and 75% female. More than half (52.5%) of the 119 learner respondents were final year university students, while 47.5% were year two and year one students.

A majority of learner respondents (93%) had learnt Mandarin before; less than half (43%) had learnt Mandarin in the last 6 years, while 13% of the learner respondents stated they had studied Mandarin more than 10 years ago and did not remember any Pinyin and basic Mandarin.

76% of the learner respondents mentioned their previous Mandarin study only covered basic Pinyin, listening and speaking content in comparison with 20% who had studied some basic grammar and 33% who had studied some reading and writing of Mandarin before.

The interviews were open interactions around the learners' needs, difficulties and applicable learning methods and the objective was to obtain some insights into the learners' views on these issues. The interviews were conducted in

Mandarin, with the purpose of practicing their listening and speaking skills in Mandarin as well.

3. Needs analysis on Cantonese speakers

In the interviews with Cantonese-speaking learners, participants were asked about the reasons for learning Mandarin to examine their learning motivation on a UK university Mandarin course. According to the interviewees, Mandarin is a significant language for their future, students may be studying Chinese for vocational or travel reasons, cultural/heritage or academic/interest reasons or for combinations of these, as the following examples demonstrate:

> "I think to speak Putonghua well is very important, very useful in the future, because this skill can help me a lot on my future job" (student A).

> "To learn Putonghua well, in the future it will be an advantage for me to look for jobs" (student B).

> "The reasons for my Mandarin learning are to improve communication with my Mainland friend, and also to help me understand Chinese culture and history" (student C).

4. Learning barriers for Cantonese speakers

Cantonese is mainly used in Guangdong, Guangxi province, Hong Kong and Macau. Cantonese is widely spoken in overseas Chinese communities, such as Australia, New Zealand, the United States, and the UK (Tsung & Cruickshank, 2011). One interviewee expressed that he had not studied the language systematically before, so he found Pinyin difficult, especially the pronunciation. He also mentioned a lack of learning and practising opportunities in Hong Kong, as Hong Kong people think speaking English displays higher class and speaking Mandarin is almost identified as foreign. Moreover, student interviewees stated that it is hard to differentiate tones for Cantonese speakers, especially as Hong Kong Pinyin has nine tones while Putonghua has four tones (five tones including neutral tone).

Furthermore, the 'ong' or 'ang, eng, ung' sounds of Pinyin are hard to pronounce and the 'ch, sh, zh' sounds are hard as "there is no similar sound in Cantonese" (student D); "Putonghua has retroflex sounds such as 'zh, ch, sh, r', while Cantonese hasn't. For example: Cantonese speakers easily read 'Shanghai' as 'Songhai', and they produce all retroflex sounds with a flat tongue" (student E).

Word order is different in Mandarin and Cantonese, e.g. the adverbial modifier is placed after the verb, there is double object word order, contrary to the use of different function words, and the adjective is put in advance, such as:

> "The same two-syllable words in Cantonese and Mandarin have opposite word order. The central word of Cantonese is at the front, such as in *guests* 客人 (Mandarin) – 人客 (Cantonese); *morning* 早晨 (Mandarin) – 晨早 (Cantonese); *love* 喜歡 (Mandarin) – 歡喜 (Cantonese)" (Student E).

As Morita (2000) observes, oral presentation is a "frequent, highly routinized part of classroom life" (p. 258) in higher education settings. It is also well-known that business courses have been putting more emphasis on oral activities, such as oral presentations.

In this study, many academic Cantonese-speaking students reported a lack of active participation and speaking in classes they had previously attended. When asked to give presentations in the target language, i.e. Mandarin, these students found it especially difficult and experienced great stress. They can write, read and even listen excellently in Mandarin, but when asked to present their Mandarin oral skills, they delivered poor presentations in the target language and were usually nervous, and avoided eye contact with the audience. From the students' feedback, it can be seen that oral presentation is an approach for Mandarin competency enhancement.

Interviewed students also stated that the oral presentation practice linked employability with the Mandarin learning, so they believed it helped their future career prospects. Due to the interests and popularity of the oral presentation themes it resulted in strong learning motivation for Cantonese speakers to overcome their difficulties in learning Mandarin. The Cantonese speakers in the case study thought that Mandarin learning for real situations allowed them to "practice a lot, interact a lot – very effective and very useful for a future career" (student F).

5. A proposal for improving Mandarin learning in Cantonese speakers

According to the interviews with the Cantonese speakers on their Mandarin learning, most of the students also mentioned they had no or little contact with Mandarin speakers for practice.

Given the above findings, a new project is proposed in this paper, namely the LEC for bridging the gap between the Mandarin learners and Mandarin speakers. The target groups will be Cantonese and Mandarin speakers at University of Nottingham.

The project will include a series of workshops with themes such as 'getting to know each other better' on mutual sides between the Mandarin and Cantonese migrant groups and 'communicate with each other better' to improve mutual language competency. The proposed activities include student-led workshops for introducing features of the Cantonese and Mandarin languages, comparisons between the Cantonese and Mandarin culture, as well as student-led presentations and joint workshops run by the Cantonese and Mandarin speakers.

It is hoped that this paper can serve as a starting point, offer guidelines to improve understanding of Cantonese speakers' challenges when learning Mandarin, and increase their learning outcomes in the end.

References

Lo, L. (2014). The role of language and communication for the migrant community integration into host society: a case study on the Chinese community in UK. *Global Science & Technology (GSTF) Journal of Law and Social Sciences, 3*(2), 46-51.

Lo, L., & Chen, Y.W. (2014). A reflection on and proposal for current social support for Chinese migrant workers in the UK. *Cambridge Journal of China Studies, 9*(2), 1-7.

Morita, N. (2000). Discourse socialization through oral classroom activities in a TESL graduate program. *TESOL Quarterly, 34*(2), 279-310. http://dx.doi.org/10.2307/3587953

Shum, M.S.K., Tsung, L., & Gao, F. (2011). Teaching and learning (through) Putonghua: from the perspective of Hong Kong teachers. In L. Tsung & K. Gruickshank (eds.), *Teaching and learning Chinese in global contexts* (pp. 46-61). London, UK: Continuum International Publishing Group,.

Tsung, L., & Cruickshank, K. (2011). Emerging trends and issues in teaching and learning Chinese. In L. Tsung & K. Gruickshank (eds.), *Teaching and learning Chinese in global contexts* (pp. 1-10). London, UK: Continuum International Publishing Group.

West, R. (1994). Needs analysis in language teaching. *Language Teaching, 27*(1), 1-19. http://dx.doi.org/10.1017/S0261444800007527

Author index